T0355608

The Supermarket of the Visible

WESTERN SYDNEY
UNIVERSITY

Thinking Out Loud: The Sydney Lectures in Philosophy and Society

These annual lectures aim to be theoretical in nature, but also to engage a general audience on questions about politics and society. The lectures are organized by Western Sydney University, in collaboration with ABC Radio National, the State Library of New South Wales, and Fordham University Press.

BOOK SERIES EDITOR
Dimitris Vardoulakis

LECTURE SERIES EXECUTIVE COMMITTEE
Chair: Dimitris Vardoulakis
Diego Bubbio
Joe Gelonesi
Richard W. Morrison

The Supermarket
of the Visible

Toward a General Economy of Images

Peter Szendy

Translated by Jan Plug

FORDHAM UNIVERSITY PRESS

NEW YORK 2019

Fordham University Press gratefully acknowledges financial assistance and support provided for the publication of this book by the University of West Sydney.

This work received support from the French Ministry of Foreign Affairs and the Cultural Services of the French Embassy in the United States through their publishing assistance program.

Fordham University Press has no responsibility for the persistence or accuracy of URLs for external or third-party Internet websites referred to in this publication and does not guarantee that any content on such websites is, or will remain, accurate or appropriate.

Fordham University Press also publishes its books in a variety of electronic formats. Some content that appears in print may not be available in electronic books.

Visit us online at www.fordhampress.com.

Library of Congress Control Number: 201993219

Printed in the United States of America

21 20 19   5 4 3 2 1

First edition

CONTENTS

viii   Contents

This book began as three lectures given at the State Library of New South Wales, in Sydney, May 5, 7, and 9, 2014. They were part of the series Thinking Out Loud: The Sydney Lectures in Philosophy and Society, organized by Dimitris Vardoulakis for the University of Western Sydney and broadcast on ABC Radio National.

Tes yeux, illuminés ainsi que des boutiques . . .
Usent insolemment d'un pouvoir emprunté
Sans connaître jamais la loi de leur beauté

Your eyes, as bright as boutiques . . .
Haughtily use a borrowed power
Never knowing the law of their own beauty

—BAUDELAIRE, "Spleen et ideal,"
poem XXV of *Les Fleurs du mal*

To me, the perfect film is as though it were
unwinding behind your eyes, and your eyes
were projecting it themselves.

—JOHN HUSTON

Sydney Lectures

Money, or The Other Side of Images

I would like to dedicate these three lectures* to the memory of Helen Tartar, former Editorial Director of Fordham University Press.

I owe her so much, I have so many cherished memories with her—in Paris, in New York, at Yale . . .

If Helen were here with us, I imagine she would be knitting. It's what she always did when listening to someone speak, and I think for her it was a way of lending an ear while occupying herself with something else. Of lending an ear *even more*, *because* apparently busying herself with something else. I find it difficult not to think of listening in general as the delicate work Helen did in tying threads, interlacing them distractedly.

*I have rewritten and developed them a great deal, while also maintaining their overall structure and often their oral form. Here and there I have also added ▷ additional features that punctuate them. That mimic, in the medium of the book, the trajectories of the gaze that belong to the DVD.

I spoke about these lectures with Helen in the Fall of 2013 in a little Manhattan restaurant, evoking them with the title I then imagined I would give them, *The Aesthetic Supermarket*. In the end, I decided to narrow the field, to close (provisionally) certain sensorial aisles or departments of the sensible in that big supermarket I first had in mind: It would be a question, not of the aesthetic as a whole, not of the *aisthēsis* that for the Greeks named sensation in general (whatever the sense organ), but of visibility alone.[1] The market and the commodification of visibility: That is what I will deal with in these three lectures.

And I will do so in an approach that I will call *iconomic*, signaling with this portmanteau that what is at stake is the circulation and economic value of images. Indeed, in *iconomy*, we hear, on the one hand, the icon (*eikōn*, one of the Greek names for the image) and, on the other, *oikonomia*, which already for Xenophon and Aristotle designated good, sound management of exchange.

Before turning to the economy of the visible, I would nonetheless like to say a few words about the big aesthetic supermarket I had in mind. For its idea or shadow will never leave us.

What I was thinking of was of course not simply some shopping mall specializing in aesthetic treatments or the sale of cosmetic products (although the shopping mall will be of great interest to us as a filmic commonplace we see staged in Jean-Luc Godard, as we do in Brian de Palma or Quentin Tarantino).[2] Rather, to speak of an aesthetic supermarket was, on the one hand, a way of indicating that *aisthēsis*, sensation or sense perception, is indeed a market in which exchange takes place: Images and sounds circulate there, as do listening, gazes, and points of view. (Moreover, perhaps it is the intrinsically exchangist quality of sensibility or sensationality, perhaps it is this exchange market that is always already there within the sensible that makes possible what we will have to describe as its unprecedented commodification in the era of globalized capitalism.)

But to speak of an aesthetic super-market (intentionally separating the prefix from the root with a hyphen) was also, on the other hand, a way of recalling that this market of the sensible could be considered a structure that is *superimposed* upon the market *tout court*. I am thinking, of course, of the famous phrase in which Marx, in the preface to his *Critique of Political Economy*, spoke of a "real base [*reale Basis*]", that is, the economic relations of production on which a "superstructure [*Überbau*]" is built or constructed, and which this sphere of *aisthēsis* would be a part of, along with the group of forms described pell-mell as "legal, political, religious, artistic, or philosophical."[3] The sensible supermarket of our sensations, in short, would be a market of senses or sensorial perceptions erected on top of the market *tout court*. And would be determined, conditioned by it, as Marx indicates when he writes that "the mode of production of material life conditions [*bedingt*] the general social, political and intellectual life process [*Lebensprozeß*]" (263).

In other words, how we perceive—see, hear, feel—is said to be the product or reflection of underlying economic and social relations. Marx suggests this very early, and absolutely explicitly, in his *1844 Manuscript*: "The abolition [*Aufhebung*] of private property," that is, upheavals in the economic base, he says, would have consequences in the very system of sensoriality, since they would lead to a "complete emancipation of all human senses [*Sinne*]" that would free them from their "alienation [*Entfremdung*]."[4]

Two pages later, Marx makes the striking and pithy assertion that our senses are *constructed*: "The forming [or construction: *Bildung*] of the five senses is a labour [*Arbeit*] of the entire history of the world [*Weltgeschichte*] down to the present" (302). Writing thus that our senses are in a sense artifacts or historically manufactured articles, Marx does not (or not yet), however, simply make them the superstructural products of an economic infrastructure. He takes the example of music: "Only [*erst*] music awakens [*erweckt*] in man the sense of music" (301). Music forms or shapes this sense, he notes, before drawing the conclusion that the senses of "social man [*gesellschaftlichen Menschen*]" are different from the senses of those who are isolated, "non-social [*ungesellschaftlichen*]" (301). Now, if it is first of all music that makes the ear, and if the musical example ought to serve here as a paradigm for the senses in general, we must conclude that the organization of sensation is not only determined by what Marx will later—in 1859—call the "real base": It is also conditioned, shaped, by artistic or aesthetic productions that belong precisely to the superstructure. Thus, it follows that objectification, objectifying externalization in general, invents and shapes sensoriality, which is constantly being reconfigured in the course of the transformation of the real by a human labor that is sedimented in it. Marx formulates this as follows, in a particularly dense and sinuous sentence:

> Only through the objectively unfolded richness of man's essential being [*erst durch den gegenständlich entfalteten Reichtum des menschlichen Wesens*] is the richness of subjective *human* sensibility [*Sinnlichkeit*] (a musical ear, an eye for beauty of form—in short, *senses* capable of human pleasure [*Genüsse*], senses affirming themselves as essential powers [*Wesenskräfte*] of *man*) either cultivated or brought into being [*teils erst ausgebildet, teils erst erzeugt*]. For not only the five senses but also the so-called mental senses, the practical senses (will, love, etc.), in a word, *human* sense, the human nature [*Menschlichkeit*] of the senses, comes to be by virtue of *its* object, by virtue of *humanised* nature.[5]

Our sense organs, in short, are never "immediate organs [*unmittelbaren Organen*]," as Marx puts it a few paragraphs earlier, but rather "*social* organs" (300). They form a divided and shared sensorium: a division or distribution of the sensible.[6]

If Marx could write that music constructs the ear, I wonder what he would have said about the gaze and film, about cinema, which he didn't have the chance to discover (the first projection by the Lumière brothers took place twelve years after his death).

For my part, I will interrogate the cinematographic construction of sight and visibility. And through cinema I will attempt to think what I therefore propose to call an iconomy.

What does this mean? And why cinema?

Even if the word is obviously a recently invented neologism, the idea of an iconomy comes from long ago, much longer ago than cinema. It goes back at least to what Marie-José Mondzain describes, in the context of the iconoclastic crisis in Byzantium, as an "iconic economy."[7] Inherited from Paul, who used it notably in the Letter to the Ephesians (1:10 and 3:9), the word *oikonomia* takes on the meaning of "incarnation" in Christian theology, since this incarnation is part of the program of Providence, that is, of divine government or economic management. And this *oikonomia* will become the very battlefield of a war of images: In the eyes of the icono-clasts, the host or "eucharist," as the incarnation of Christ, is the only "non-deceiving" icon, that is, the "truthful image of the carnal economy of Christ-God" (as decreed by the Council of Hieria, summoned by Constan-tine V in 754).[8] Thus, as Mondzain demonstrates with great rigor, "All these aspects of the incarnational economy will be found in full again in the iconic economy" (32), that is, in the "organization, administration, and management of all visibilities" (34). We must understand the concept of iconomy, then, beginning from this genealogical knot, this nodal point at which the respective stemmas of the image and economy cross.

But where the knot tightens and begins to configure the contours of the concept strictly speaking is in numismatics, to which Mondzain devotes a few fascinating pages. Indeed, the history of the minting of coins reflects— one is tempted to say incarnates—the iconological conflicts I just men-tioned. On the one hand, there are those who imprint the image of Christ on their coins, as Emperor Justinian II was the first to do during his first reign (from 685 to 695); on the other hand, there are those who, like the iconoclasts Leo III and his son Constantine V, renounce all representation of Christ, and even go so far as to remove the cross. These numismatic practices, Mondzain writes, "clearly show the connection between the ico-nography and the founding signs of both economic life and political insti-tutions on objects whose essence is circulation itself" (157). Thus, we see emerge the concept of iconomy in the sense in which we will understand it when Mondzain writes without hesitation that the "image is therefore in the same situation as coinage itself," that it resembles "fiduciary signs that incarnate . . . the effects of faith and of credit" (158). What is affirmed, then, is what we might call the double iconomic equivalence: not only is currency made in the image of the image, but the image, in turn, is made in the image of money.

If it is true, as Mondzain says, that "we are today the heirs and propaga-tors of that iconic empire" (151) to which the Catholic faith gave birth in the economy of the flesh, this heritage took detours, routes that I cannot reconstruct here (one could, for example, consider at length the transfor-mation of the incarnation of Christ that is the host, the only true image according to the iconoclasts: Beginning at around the middle of the eleventh century, it began to be made, to be impressed *in modum denarii*, "like coins").[9] But it was important at the very least to give you a glimpse of the layers and depth of the history in which my iconomic approach is rooted.

Still, some will say that it's quite a leap from Byzantine iconoclasm to the frames of cinema. And why restrict our inquiry into iconomy to film, one might ask? It does seem that to do so would limit its scope to a late (a recent) invention and to a very narrow genre of images. Yet can we be so certain, I am tempted to respond, that this is a restriction or limitation? Isn't film, on the contrary, the name for a generalization without limit of the iconomic equivalence between the image and money?

This is what a formulation from Gilles Deleuze's *Cinema 2: The Time-Image* suggests in the most fascinating way, a formulation that we will be reading and re-reading constantly: "Money," he writes, "is the reverse of *all* the images that the cinema shows and edits on the front."[10] We are going to listen to the resonances of this formulation, to its context, to its ramifications. We will auscultate and unfold it in as many ways as possible. But we can already say, following Deleuze, that it is indeed *all* images that, with cinema, have become the recto of a monetary verso that they carry structurally inscribed on their back.

Yes, *all* images, for cinema is for Deleuze much more than the name of a technical mechanism that was developed from the Lumière brothers' projections in 1895. It is no more or less than *the name of the world* ("the universe," Deleuze writes in reading Bergson, "as cinema in itself, a meta-cinema").[11] And from this develops a series of abyssal questions that promises to open beneath each step in our filmic approach to iconomy. What, in fact, are we to understand by "cinema" in Deleuze's formulation about money forming the other side of all cinema's images? What sense will we have to give this formulation that seems destined to oscillate, to fluctuate wildly, between a meaning one might want to confine to the restricted economy of film and a hyperbolic meaning that would lead us toward a general iconomy that would encompass the universe?

So many questions that will also amount to wondering, in tune with our brief traversal of Marx's *1844 Manuscript*: Is there a market of the visible that would precede, that would exceed, the commerce of images in the supposedly strict sense of the word? Is there a bigger market, an arche-economy, of images, in other words, a super- or hyper-market of visibility that would be the counterpart (the "reverse") of the metacinema that for Deleuze is the world.

Let's leave these questions aside and pretend, for a while, that we believe Deleuze is talking about cinema in the common sense when he writes (and we will re-read the sentence again and again): "Money is the reverse of all the images that the cinema shows and edits on the front."

How are we to understand this sentence?

One is of course tempted to see in it the echo of what numerous films by Godard show explicitly, that is, that the task of cinema is to *give an account* of its own conditions of production. Or better: that its task is to be *account-able* (which is also to say, responsible) for itself.

Thus, just after the opening credits in *All's Well* ("a film directed by Jean-Luc Godard and Jean-Pierre Gorin," 1972), just after this minute and a half that is punctuated by the sound of a clapper board and voices count-ing off the takes (*"All's Well*, 3B second take"), we hear the male voice-over say, "I want to make a film." The female voice responds, "Making a film takes money." And the film then shows the expenditures that make it pos-sible: Each director (Godard, Gorin) gets a check made out in a percentage

("eleven and a half percent" for their "directing"); then "seven thousand Francs" for the "script," "sixty-six thousand Francs" for the "cinematogra-phy," "twenty-three thousand nine hundred Francs" for the "sound," "thirty-eight thousand eight hundred Francs" for the "assistants," etc. Every role passes by, including the "minor roles" ("one hundred and thirty thousand three hundred Francs") and "extras" ("sixty-four thousand one

 hundred and two Francs"), ending with "social secu-
rity contributions" ("one hundred ninety-three thou-
sand eight hundred and twenty-two Francs") and
"contingencies" ("ten percent"). Each time, a thumb
and an index finger take hold of the check in the
upper right corner of the screen and tear it from the
checkbook, leafing through it slowly and monoto-
nously: a sort of folioscope or flip-book that verges
on making the film coincide with the peeling of the checks out of the
checkbook.

The dialogue between the two voices of the voice-over continues as the
names of the stars appear. "Yves Montand," we read on the screen, while
the female voice says, "If you get some stars, they'll give us money." And
the male voice responds, "Good, then we'll just have to get some stars."
The leafing resumes for a moment ("twenty-three percent" for an "international star," we read on one of the two checks that remain to be paid), when
the female voice asks, "And what are you going to tell Yves Montand and
Jane Fonda? Because actors, if they're going to accept, need a story." And so
the story also seems to be part of the market, a sort of credit or advance on
the film. "A love story, generally speaking," concludes the female voice,
punctuated by the tearing of the final remaining check, for the second
"international star," also paid "twenty-three percent."

The tempo of this sequence after the opening credits is thus that of a
monotone fiduciary inscription that makes audible, in a loop, the irritating
rubbing of the felt-tip pen on the paper and the sound of the leaves—the
checks—being torn out. What Godard repeats in every way is that the
writing of the film, that the cinematography, is in fact nothing other than
the scene of its own expenditure. In *Script for the Film "Passion"* (1982,
filmed after *Passion*), the director, at his editing table, thus goes so far as to
say that the script is in the end an invention of accounting, is made to *give
an account*:

> I think . . . we see the world first and then we write it afterwards. And the
> world that *Passion* describes, well, you have to see it first, see, see that it existed
> in order to be able to film it. And, I believe, I really believe that the first signs

of writing (Mycenae before Athens) the first traces of writing—it's shopkeepers who invented writing. . . . And besides, cinema, which copies life, cinema, which comes from life, cinema started like that: you didn't make up scripts, you didn't write them; you set out and filmed. Mark Sennett [1880–1960, nicknamed the King of Comedy in the era of silent films] in his little Hollywood studio—before it was called Hollywood—he set out with a car, a friend dressed up as a cop, a girl dressed up as a swimmer, and a young man playing the part of lover—he set out, he filmed, and then, little by little, as he had some success, he did more and more, every day; it was expensive, and then the accountant panicked because he didn't know where the money had gone. Then the accountant wrote: swimmer, 100 Francs; cop, 50 Francs; lover, 3 dollars. And then, little by little, that was it: a cop, a lover. But it was a cop in love with a swimmer who is being followed by her lover. And this came from the accounting, the script came from the accounting, was first of all a trace, a trace of how the money was spent. But first you saw it. And I wanted to see.[12]

It is precisely here that the gap will open for us between Godard's statement and Deleuze's formulation. For according to Godard, as we have read, seeing comes *before* accounting, which is but its *a posteriori* notation (posterior twice over even, since we see first and then register what we see and, finally, write the script as the account of what has already been registered). As though there were a purity of seeing, then, as though there were a visibility that is not already contaminated by the economy of accounting and that owed nothing to the market. While Deleuze will suggest that everything visible in cinema—which is also to say, if we go in the direction of a general iconomy, everything visible *tout court*—is visible only *because* money is *already there* on the reverse of every possible image or photogram.

But let's not go too quickly. After all, we still don't know what "money" means in Deleuze's formulation ("money is the reverse of all the images").

To be sure, in the sentences immediately preceding this formulation, Deleuze speaks of the "harsh law of cinema," according to which "a minute of image . . . costs a day of collective work." And he cites this pithy sentence recalled by Fellini, with its inexorable obviousness: "When there is no more money left, the film will be finished" (80). It would seem, then, that money here specifically designates the cost of filmic images. But can we be certain that Deleuze wishes to restate in turn what so many others said before him, that is, that cinematographic production entails financial means that are unheard of in other arts?

Already in 1935, in his famous essay "The Work of Art in the Age of Its Technological Reproducibility" (which we will return to at length during the third lecture), Walter Benjamin wrote:

> In film [*Bei den Filmwerken*], the technological reproducibility of the product [*die technische Reproduzierbarkeit des Produkts*] is not an externally imposed condition of its mass dissemination, as it is, say, in literature and painting [*eine von außen her sich einfindende Bedingung ihrer massenweisen Verbreitung*]. *The technological reproducibility of films is based directly* [unmittelbar begründet] *on the technology of their production. This not only makes possible the mass dissemination of films in the most direct way, but actually enforces* [erzwingt] *it.* It does so because the process of producing a film is so costly that an individual who could afford to buy a painting, for example, could not afford to buy a film. Film is a collective acquisition. It was calculated in 1927 that, in order to make a profit, a major film needed to reach an audience of nine million.[13]

We have to read closely here in order to get an accurate measure of the difference from what Deleuze suggests. For Benjamin, the technological reproducibility of film, like that of photography, is inherent in the technique of its production: Like a "photographic negative" from which "a multitude of copies can be made," each piece of movie film is intrinsically reproducible as countless copies, none of which is more "authentic [*echt*]" than any other. What is thus anchored or rooted in cinema as such is the possibility of reproducing its products ad infinitum. Cinema's relationship to money, in contrast, is not of the same kind: If the financial investment required to make a film enforces (*erzwingt*, Benjamin says) its mass distribution if it is to be paid off, this constraint, as inexorable as it is, remains extrinsic. It is not structurally inscribed in the mechanism itself (moreover, since Benjamin wrote these lines there has been no lack of examples of films produced with very modest means and that were diffused confidentially: They are still films that, as such, are reproducible through and through in the analogue or digital grain or pixels of their texture).

This is why, in the lines preceding the formulation we are trying to auscultate, Deleuze can write, without explicitly naming Benjamin but as though responding to him from the distance of a half century, "what defines industrial art is not mechanical reproduction but the internalized relation with money" (77). Yet if money is thus for Deleuze "the most intimate and most indispensable enemy" of cinema (77), if money comes to take the constitutive place that Benjaminian reproducibility held within the filmic mechanism, it is in that it does not only name the cost of cinema's images. It does not merely designate the considerable investments that certain sequences require (in the final credits of some super-productions, the list of those who worked on the special effects sometimes looks like the census for an entire city!), any more than it does the profits that this or that image can generate, thanks to "product placements" in films, for example.[14] Money, rather, inhabits film even before it is distributed: It is

▷ *Merchandise: Godzilla's Eye*

lodged in its innermost texture; it is so inherent in it that when one attempts to show it, to make it visible, one exposes film itself, film as such.

Let's reread Deleuze's formulation, then, as it moves, in the remainder of the sentence, toward its immediate consequences: "Money is the reverse of all the images that the cinema shows and edits on the front, so that films about money are already, if *implicitly*, films within the film or about the film" (my emphasis). Money, we see, resides in the slightest *folds* of film (the implicit, from the Latin *implicare*, is what is folded into . . .). And to understand what money is the name of here, we must now turn to those foldings of film upon film.

To where film looks at itself. Where it attempts to cast a glance—but which?—at its iconomic other side.

The fourth season of the famous television series *The Sopranos* opened on September 15, 2002, with a remarkable episode titled "For All Debts Public and Private." The title is borrowed, as it were, from the phrase that figures on all American banknotes: "This note is legal tender for all debts, public and private."

At the end of the episode, Tony Soprano's nephew, Christopher Moltisanti, visits his mother after having avenged the death of his father by assassinating the police lieutenant who killed him. Chris has thus settled a blood debt. And he carries with him the twenty-dollar bill he made a point of taking from the wallet on the cop's corpse. As his mother sits at the table facing the framed portrait of his departed father, Chris stands in front of the kitchen refrigerator, which is covered in photographs, religious images, and popular proverbs printed on a background of kitschy twilight or rainbow colors. "Keep it simple," one of them says. "One day at a time," states another.[15]

Chris uses magnets to attach the twenty-dollar bill he is carrying to this latter maxim as the soundtrack plays the percussive opening of the song that will accompany the closing credits.[16] The sound of cowbells that marks the tempo almost gets confused with the ticking of a clock measuring the passing time. And in fact, the result of the collage Chris makes before our very eyes is to isolate the word *Time*, which is apposed to the bill, as though the proverbial expression were transformed into a different one, except that the verb *to be* is elided: *Time (is) Money*. In the context of this episode, whose title is borrowed from fiduciary money, it is tempting to translate this by *Time is Debt*. For time—and I will return to this—is not only money; it is also and no doubt above all credit.

Cut. The editing brings us back to the mother, who is sitting. In the meantime, during the exchange the son has just completed in his brief trafficking in signs (at once linguistic, pictorial, and monetary), the image of the father has been turned over. We see the back of the frame, the black

back of the portrait, now lying down, its front against the table. Chris looks silently at his mother one last time, while the camera moves in for a close-up of the banknote, as though the image of Andrew Jackson, the seventh president of the United States, had come to take the place of the overturned father. Or as though the reverse of the image, its other face, was, precisely, money.

The episode then finishes by zooming in slowly and inexorably on the eyes at the center of the bill. Is it because it is a bit wrinkled, because there is a slight fold across it, that the gaze emanating from the money seems cross-eyed?

Let's keep this gaze in mind, for we will have occasion to speak of it again later, of what is squinting [*louche*] in the folds. Of what is shady [*louche*] in the folded iconomy of the fiduciary image.

The image and its reverse, the image and money, the image and debt, the image and time: This is what the Deleuzian iconomic formulation we are attempting to listen to demands that we think. Let's reread it in its complete form: "Money is the reverse of all the images that the cinema shows and edits on the front, so that films about money are already, if implicitly, films within the film or about film."

Around these words in *Time-Image* revolves a constellation of filmmakers and films that have tried to put on screen this verso of filmic images, to thematize their monetary reverse: Wim Wenders, Marcel L'Herbier, and of course Robert Bresson, whose last film, *L'Argent* (*Money*), which was made in 1983, perhaps allows us to see the allegory par excellence of this fiduciary background that, hiding behind each film image, makes it possible.

So what happens at the very beginning of *Money?* The door of an ATM closes, becoming the metal background, the black screen, on which is traced a writing in light, where luminescent streaks (reflections of the headlights of cars passing in the street) stream past, and  the white characters of the credits are displayed, as though this open and then closed door were the condition of possibility of all the images to come. The first shot then shows one glass door forming an angle with another one. A boy (Norbert) approaches, knocks on the glass, and opens the door. It is the beginning of the month; he has come to ask his father for his allowance. The bills then pile up on his father's desk, as though we were seeing for a moment the reemergence in the plot, that is, in the diegetic space, of the fiduciary currency that the initial closing of the ATM seemed to want to

> *Deleted Scenes:* Doors and Slide Changers in *Pickpocket* and *Obsession*

confine to the extradiegetic, outside the film and as what makes it possible. But when Norbert asks for more money—he has to pay off a debt he ran up at his high school—his father refuses. And we see the glass door of the office close, repeating thus the film's opening gesture.[17]

We will have to wait a long time for the image of the ATM door, for *Money*'s very first image, to be truly taken up again and included in the story told to us, that is, fully integrated and justified in the diegesis. It is only after Yvon's arrest and trial that we see Lucien and his two followers traffic in credit cards. Bresson then once again shows the same metal panel that slides open and closed; then the machine freezes, gets blocked, keeping the customer's card, after Lucien has made a point of memorizing the code. When Lucien then takes the card out with a pair of pliers and puts it into the ATM, the camera focuses at length on the bills coming out: five one-hundred Franc bills—so-called "Delacroix," after Eugène Delacroix, whose self-portrait, as well as a detail of his *Liberté guidant le peuple*, are printed on their back—are issued one after the other, like so many images that have just reintroduced, on the recto of the film and in the world of its narration, something that to that point had remained hidden, in a background or backworld.

Money, in Bresson's *Money*, appears at first as the ground of every possible filmic image. Then, moving from this transcendental ground to the empirical plane of the story, it is printed, cut up, and distributed in the form of notes [*coupures*][18] that are so many images among other images.[19]

Michel, the protagonist of Bresson's masterly *Pickpocket* (1959), has the impossible task of attempting to take hold of this money, which seems to slip *between images*, moving from film to its outside, and vice versa, as we see in the rightly famous sequence in the train in the Gare de Lyon.

Michel climbs into the train car whose aisle, which passes between two parallel rows of windows that overlook the platform on the outside and the interior of the compartments respectively, is like a sliding channel for a continuous procession or scrolling. He steals the wallet of a passenger and passes it to his accomplice (portrayed in the film by a real pickpocket, Henri Kassagi, who would later become a famous magician and conjurer). The wallet is relayed to a second accomplice and in this way passes from hand to hand; it circulates along the aisle, while the image of the pickpockets working in a chain is doubled and reflected in the compartment windows.

When another victim walks through the narrow aisle, it is as though the bodies have to submit to a certain flattening to make the exchanges and their comings and goings easier (Bresson himself recalled with relish his "obsession with flattening all images," "as though with a clothes iron," to make the transactions or transformations between them easier).[20] Filmed head on from inside a compartment, the torso we see from the front and the one we see from behind are like two sliding panels, like two slide changers [*passe-vues*][21] that ensure that the images change within the lantern—a magic lantern in more than one sense—that this windowed car is. The victim's chest, clothed in a suit, seems to be flattened onto the plane of the screen, and the gap between his jacket and shirt is compressed into nothing more than two stacked plates between which one might slip a still or a slide.

We find this same barely layered flatness of the passageway again in so many other moments in *Pickpocket*, where the slide changer, the infra-thin [*infra-mince*][22] gap between the surface of the screen and itself, can become the fold in a newspaper, a piece of clothing that falls open, or a door that remains ajar. I am thinking in particular of the famous opening sequence in the Longchamp hippodrome: Michel, viewed from behind, is on his way to the racetrack and joins the crowd of spectators, which the camera then films head on, frontally, as though better to flatten them into a fresco or compress them into a bas-relief that takes up the entire foreground, in whose flatness fingers thread and banknotes-images circulate. Just as Michel is about to slip the money he has pulled out of the bag of the woman next to him into his own pocket, a man passes by with a newspaper, making the paper money disappear as though by means of a wipe (as English has it, as though one were wiping off or effacing the image). The money is thus *spirited away* twice: It is taken by the hand in the bag and almost immediately erased from the surface of the screen by the wipe [*volet*] that doubles the theft [*vol*].

Once we pay attention to them, we notice the folded newspapers found everywhere in *Pickpocket*, where they are so many opportunities for an image, part of an image, to move into or under another, to be exchanged with it, thanks to this folding of the visible that opens obscure transactions within it. Think, for example, of the sequence in the subway, when a fascinated Michel watches another pickpocket in action ("a man acting strangely, whom I couldn't take my eyes off," says his narrating voice-over). The newspaper first serves as a visual mask covering the manual operations of extracting a wallet. This wallet is then carried away, hidden in the folds of the newspaper, from which, in a fadeout, it will reemerge in another space and in other hands: no longer in the subway, but in Michel's room, where we see him practicing the movements he just observed in another. Thus, the folded newspaper in a sense becomes the allegory for filmic montage itself, as the passage from one shot to the next, situated elsewhere.

At Michel's, in his room, it seems clear that the folded newspaper, the piece of clothing that falls open, and the door that one cracks open are all

passages into which the banknote image can be slid, so that it can be spirited away and exchanged with another. Thus, when Michel later practices undoing a watchband from the leg of a table, we see him slip the watch between his bedspring and mattress before standing up to go pull the door shut with a delicate gesture of his index and middle fingers that is identical in every way to the gesture with which he opens jackets. In an extremely subtle shot, Bresson then shows the ajar door caught in the shadow cast by the open jacket Michel is in the process of putting on.

A door half-open, clothing that falls open, the gap between the mattress and the box spring, a folded newspaper: These are all so many interstices that introduce a slight stratification into the projection surface, where a banknote can disappear and then reappear. These gaps, these crevices, these folds remark, in the story, in the filmic diegesis, the streaming of images, that is, the metadiegetic slide changers that make the film possible.

It is as though, in these cracks or fissures, the cineworld were to open a crack to its reverse, allowing us to glimpse its conditions of possibility. For what we would find on the verso of each image is no doubt nothing other than the principle of its interchangeability, that is, its potential to circulate, destined as it is to enter into transactions: In short, its pure exchange value, which, Bresson never stops emphasizing, is what is most proper to cinematography.

"The value of an image must be, above all, an exchange value," he declares.[23] And he notes elsewhere: "Cinematographic film, where the images, like the words in a dictionary, have no power and value except through their position and relation."[24] Or again: "No absolute value in an image" (11). Which seems to be able to become a *cinematographic* image only on the condition that it is "taken . . . in such a way that it has above all an exchange value."

This is perhaps what Michel and the other pickpockets try to grasp, then, under the name or sign of money: exchange as such, the—disappearing, par excellence—instant of pure exchange, which is to be taken, if possible, to be caught as it flies past, that it might be pulled from the obscurity into which it falls again and again, without end.

Money, in short, is the name of the passing of images as they are exchanged within the slide changer.

We no doubt understand a bit better now what money might mean in the Deleuzian formulation that has led us to watch all these sequences from Bresson: If "money is the reverse of all the images that the cinema shows and edits on the front," it is because it is another name for that "exchange value" that, as Bresson put it, makes images cinematographic, that grants them their filmicity. In other words, for there to be film, images, like money, must be exchangeable.

But Deleuze goes further and shows that this exchange hides another one. "Money is time," he adds, inserting into the paragraph that immediately follows the statement of his iconomic formulation the same proverbial expression that Chris, at the end of the *Sopranos* episode, stuck on his mother's fridge. Deleuze turns and returns this phrase, whose origin disappears into an immemorial past. Using the best-known and most common form of the saying ("time is money"), he writes that "time [is] money or the circulation of money." Or, reversing the direction of the equivalence: "It is what undermines cinema, the old malediction: money is time."[25]

▷ *Deleted Scenes*: Three Variations on Time and Money (Antonioni, De Palma, Bresson)

How to understand the iconomic meaning of this proverb that Deleuze makes pivot by exchanging its two sides: Time is money or money is time?

Money is the name of that which from the beginning virtualizes, spirits away, or phantomizes every image, so that it is never simply present but is henceforth always exchangeable, ready to be substituted for by another image, including a copy of itself. The scene in the train in the Gare de Lyon in *Pickpocket* already suggested this. Let's return to it, then.

The scene, as we recall, is structured along two axes. On one hand, the axis of the aisle the flattened travelers pass through, travelers who are also the bearers of flat images that circulate by slipping one after the other into those slide changers that are the pieces of clothing (the equivalent of the folds in the newspapers or the half-open doors). And on the other hand, the perpendicular axis of the compartments. Each of the images is immediately doubled in the compartment windows, like a mirror reflection. Actual images that pass by while giving birth to their virtual doubles: This is exactly what Deleuze called "the crystal image" in the pages of *Time-Image* around which we are circling.

What does this mean?

Deleuze constructs this concept on the basis of Bergson's analysis of memory, which he appropriates for, and in a sense transposes to, cinema. Bergson asserts that memory is not formed once perception is complete, as though memory were waiting for perception to be finished to be able to begin.[26] We cannot "split our psychological life" in this way, he says: Instead, memory has to be thought of as like the "shadow" of the perception "outlined at its sides," created "gradually along with perception itself." In short, as Bergson writes in a crucial passage to which Deleuze returns several times, each time citing several lines:

> Our actual existence, then, whilst it is unrolled in time, duplicates itself all along with a virtual existence, a mirror-image. Every moment of our life presents two aspects, it is actual and virtual, perception on the one side and memory on the other. Each moment of life is split up as and when it is posited. Or rather, it consists in this very splitting, for the present moment, always going forward, the fleeting limit between the immediate past which is now no more and the immediate future which is not yet, would be a mere abstraction were it not the moving mirror which continually reflects perception as memory. (165)

This "moving mirror" is quite precisely what Deleuze re-baptizes with the name *crystal*. And the fourth chapter of *Time-Image*, the chapter we are reading and in which our iconomic formulation appears, opens with a whole series of evocations of mirrors in films: "The image in the mirror," Deleuze notes, "is virtual in relation to the actual character that the mirror catches" (70).

We could add to the mirror scenes Deleuze mentions briefly (in Losey, in Welles . . .) that of the train car in the Gare de Lyon in *Pickpocket*. There we would see at once an allegory of Bergson's conception of memory and an allegory of the cinematographic mechanism itself. Image-perceptions, actual images, pass by in the slide changer of the aisle, and they are all reflected in the mirror of the compartment windows, immediately forming a memory-image, immediately becoming a virtual image. In short, Bresson's filmic train car is a good example of what Deleuze calls "these consolidates of actual and virtual which define a crystalline structure (in a general, aesthetic, rather than a scientific, sense)" (73).

But what exactly happens with that money that I said *virtualizes* every image? And how is our iconomic formulation about the monetary reverse of images articulated with the Deleuzian concept of the crystal or of the crystal-image, whose origin in Bergson I just traced briefly? Put differently: how does one go, in the middle of the chapter we are concerned with, from "money is the reverse of all images" to "money is time"?

Money, I said first of all with Bresson, is the name of the "exchange value" of images within the cinematographic slide changer: Money is that exchangeability that allows images to pass by in the flattened aisle of the train car–cinema. But now it is a different exchange that we see constantly produced and reproduced in the Deleuzian crystal-image, as we do in the abyssal mirroring of the compartment windows: no longer an exchange between an actual image and the image that follows, but between the actual and the virtual. "In fact the crystal," Deleuze writes, "constantly exchanges the two distinct images which constitute it, the actual image of the present which passes and the virtual image of the past which is preserved" (85). And this exchange, this crystalline exchange, grounds, makes possible, the other exchange, that of the scrolling in which an actual image takes the place of the preceding one as the sights pass. Put differently, it is *because* the actual images are virtualized that they can let others take their place, can allow themselves to be substituted for by others:

> What is actual is always a present. . . . It is clearly necessary for it to pass on for the new present to arrive, and it is clearly necessary for it to pass at the same time as it is present, at the moment that it is present. Thus the image has to be present and past, still present and already past, at one and at the same time. If it was not already past at the same time as present, the present would never pass on. . . . The present is the actual image, and *its* contemporaneous past is the virtual image, the image in a mirror. (79)

The condition of exchange (of passage) in the aisle of the slide changer, Deleuze says in short, is exchange (passage) in the mobile mirror of time.

Now, if money is the name of the first exchange, it seems to be the name of the second one as well, which makes the first possible. Indeed, when Deleuze, just after his iconomic formulation on the monetary reverse of images, in turn takes up the dictum "time is money," when he turns and returns it, backwards and forwards, he glosses it thus:

> This is the old curse that undermines cinema: money is time. . . . Time is by nature the conspiracy of unequal exchange or the impossibility of an equivalence. It is in this sense that it is money. (77–78, translation modified)

In short, Deleuze says that money is time or time is money to the extent that it is the crystalline exchange of the actual and virtual. And it is this exchange that, for reasons that remain to be elucidated, Deleuze qualifies as "dissymmetrical, unequal and without equivalence" (81).

Why is this second exchange, which is really first or foundational, placed under the sign of inequality or inequivalence?

Let's read the rest of the passage we have begun reading:

> Time is by nature the conspiracy of unequal exchange or the impossibility of an equivalence. It is in this sense that it is money: in Marx's two formulations, C-M-C is that of equivalence, but M-C-M' is that of impossible equivalence or tricked, dissymmetrical exchange. (77–78, translation modified)

With the first formulation—someone sells a commodity (C) for money (M) in order to buy another commodity (C)—Marx describes the situation in which products exchanged by means of the intermediary of currency are "equivalents," their "equal value [*Gleichwert*]" being the very "condition of the normal course [*Bedingung des normalen Verlaufs*]" of exchange.[27] However, with the second formulation—one invests money (M) in a commodity (C) in order to resell it at a higher price (M')—the exchange produces an "excess" that Marx proposes calling "surplus value [*Mehrwert*]." Thus, he notes, the initial value "adds to itself [*verwertet sich*]"; that is, it is transformed into "capital." The exchange is thus no longer worthy of its name. (Was it ever? This is the whole question I will return to in the next lecture.) The exchange is distorted by the "inflation which time puts into the exchange" (78), as Deleuze puts it.

We must remember here that beginning with *Anti-Oedipus*, Deleuze and Guattari insisted on thinking economics on the basis not of exchange but debt. They saw in Nietzsche's second essay in *On the Genealogy of Morality* an "attempt—and a success without equal—at interpreting primitive economy in terms of debt, in the debtor-creditor relationship, by eliminating every consideration of exchange." Money in their eyes was first and foremost "the means for rendering the debt infinite."[28]

What happens, then, when this economic discourse on impossible—or the fiction of—exchange is transposed, translated, into the field of iconomy? I am of course not talking about what certain film scripts thematize when they *recount*, for example, that "money, because it is of the order of time, makes impossible any reparation for evil done, any equivalence or just retribution" (this is in a sense the short summary that Deleuze offers of the plot of Bresson's final work) (*Time-Image*, 81). I am not talking, therefore, about what film is the narrative or narration of, but about the properly and structurally iconomic consequences of Deleuze's discourse on unequal, dissymmetrical exchange: Just as money was the "reverse of *all* the images" of cinema (let me emphasize: yes, *all* the images, including those that do not show money), in what way are inequivalence and debt inscribed on the back of each frame, including in films that in no way deal with debt?

Deleuze doesn't really say, and he even seems to hesitate. For if the crystal-image is indeed defined as that mobile mirror in which the actual image and the virtual image are exchanged, the nature of the exchange in question is uncertain. Sometimes, as we have read, it is described as dissymmetrical, unequal, without equivalent; and sometimes, on the contrary, as "mutual" (and then Deleuze speaks of a "mutual image"), that is, as putting in play "a front [the actual] and its reverse [the virtual], which are totally reversible" (*Time-Image*, 72–73, translation modified).[29] This hesitation verges on paradox or aporia in the following passage, part of which we have just read, where the adjective "mutual" almost appears in an apposition as a synonym for "unequal":

In fact the crystal constantly exchanges the two distinct images which constitute it, the actual image of the present which passes and the virtual image of
the past which is preserved. . . . This is unequal exchange. . . , the mutual
image. (85)

But there is absolutely no lack of consequence or incoherence on
Deleuze's part here. For this hesitant oscillation, which sometimes tips the
exchange toward mutuality or reciprocity (toward exchange properly
speaking, then) and sometimes toward dissymmetry or inequivalence
(toward the impossibility of exchange), this tension is quite precisely what
affects the punctiformity of the present, which at once contracts into an
indivisible point and yet deviates from itself, tightens into the instant at the
same time that it doubles itself:[30]

> The actual image and *its* virtual image thus constitute the smallest internal
> circuit, ultimately a peak or point, but a physical point which has distinct
> elements [a point, then, that paradoxically would be divided]. . . . Distinct,
> but indiscernible, such are the actual and the virtual which are in continual
> exchange. (73)

The point of the punctiform present thus holds together the actual and
the virtual; the punctiformity of the now [*maintenant*] maintains them in
their indiscernibility, in the mutuality of their reciprocal co-belonging. But
this is a point that is immediately or at the same time divided, stretched, and
extended in the space of its disparity from itself. If the actual and the virtual
are *in continual exchange*, moreover, it is because their exchange is precisely
never fulfilled or completed, because it is always deferred. And that is why
Deleuze insists on saying that their exchange is "started again" (74), that the
"crystal-image thus receives the principle which is its foundation: *endlessly
relaunching exchange which is dissymmetical*" (81; emphasis added).[31]

In short, if exchange is *constant*, that is, *constantly* put off until later, it is
because time, that is, money, never stops working in the back of the image,
such that it never coincides with itself.

Exchangeability thus turns out to be the at once crucial and problematic
category of what I will continue to call *iconomy*. Indeed, I will have to undertake a questioning auscultation of exchangeability in the next lecture.

But I don't want to close this first lecture without returning, as promised, to the image of the twenty-dollar bill at the end of the *Sopranos* episode titled "For All Debts Public and Private." As you recall, once the photographic image of the father is turned over to show its back, and once the money is put up beside the word *time*, fiduciary money itself looks at us eye to eye.

As I said, this gaze that addresses us seems to be cross-eyed, to suffer from exotropia. It seems to be staring at us, perpendicular to the screen, with its right eye. And with the left, at the edge of the fold across the note, it seems to want to look elsewhere, maybe right into the plane of the screen, that is, into the screen's depth, at once layered and flat, where images pass by one after the other. We thus find ourselves before a look *of* money (understood at once as an objective and subjective genitive, for money here is the object that we see and the subject, so to speak, who sees), we find ourselves before a double vision that, from the verso of images, seems to want to see and the film as we see it, and the film as it *would see* itself taking place, as if it could look at itself *in the very axis of its temporality*.

With one eye (its right), this gaze that might be called iconomic looks at the punctiform present of the image that finds itself in the slide changer: It looks at that image—a different image every time—in whose presence the actual and the virtual exchange places in mutual reciprocity. It looks at the film.

But with the other eye (the left), it looks into the folded (lack of) depth of becoming, where there is no exchange worthy of the name, only dissymmetry, advance and delay, credit and debt. It looks at the film in film.[32]

This is why the gaze *of* money—*of* time—squints.

The Point of (No) Exchange, or The Debt-Image

After our patient and minute reading of Deleuze's iconomic discourse, I would like to propose a different experience of thinking that, I hope, will bring a smile to your face, make you laugh.

Imagine the following scene, whether from film or life: I'm sure it sometimes happens to you as it does to me that, walking briskly down the street, you come upon pedestrians walking in the opposite direction, also at a diligent pace. You're walking around, they're walking around, everything seems fluid; you manage to avoid one another, that is, to allow one another to go by without slowing down by deviating just enough, each of you making a small symmetrical deviation from the other. But from time to time things get stuck. The fluidity gets blocked, you step aside in the wrong direction, the same direction as the person coming toward you, so that, instead of allowing that person to pass by at the same time you do, you find yourself nose-to-nose, obstacle against obstacle. It can be embarrassing, running into each other, into a perfect stranger. It's often quite comical, all the more so since, generally when it happens, it seems to want to repeat itself immediately in a loop, like a jump cut that would force the two characters of this banal sequence repeatedly to find themselves in front of one another, getting in the way of continuing their walk despite all their attempts to be kind and courteous.

What happens in this scene, this arche-scene, we have all experienced?

It is clearly a matter of *cadence*, of rhythm, a matter of the conformity or adjustment of the rhythms of walking.[1] But we can imagine how this basic combination of two approaches that attempt to compromise, to come to terms with each other, could be magnified and developed, the degree of complexity it would reach if one added not only a third walker but a grid of footmarks, a network of marks—or steps—on which your feet had to fall.

This is exactly what we observe in a hilarious sequence in Jacques Tati's *Mon Oncle* (1958). Monsieur Arpel drags Pichard, his faithful underling, into a conversation punctuated by their steps across paving

stones of various sizes that partially cover the loose gravel of the hyper-modern villa's garden. The subject of their muttering—Tati himself, in the person of Monsieur Hulot—silently joins the steps of the boss and his employee, sketching a three-way dance that tends to stall, to get blocked at every step. And that ends when Monsieur Arpel, facing Monsieur Hulot, who is walking backward, exclaims in a burst of barely contained impatience, "Go around, old chap!"

They end up getting by, then, but the fluidity of movement constantly risks coming to a standstill, getting blocked. In short, what the arche-scene I am speaking about and on which Tati offers a virtuoso variation demands that we think is that punctuation, the punctuating gesture or the punctuation mark, is always involved wherever there is the possibility of a passage ("Go around [*passez*], old chap!," Arpel says to Hulot), that is, the possibility of a change or exchange.

It is such a *point of exchange* (if there is one, and nothing could be less certain) that I would like to try to take up. And to try to define it, I suggest we turn to other scenes of trading places in which the moment of exchange is clearly in question.

We find the equivalent of these blocked steps in *Mon Oncle*—but transposed higher up this time, elevated to the level of the hands, which is to say, taken to the level of exchange par excellence that is barter—in an equally hilarious scene from *The Party*, Blake Edwards's 1968 film. Thanks to a misunderstanding, Hrundi V. Bakshi (Peter Sellers) finds himself at a party given by a rich Hollywood producer, Fred Clutterbuck. And in Clutterbuck's luxurious house, Bakshi pushes the buttons on a control panel, setting into motion the table on which the guests have set their glasses, plates, jugs, and ashtrays. Just as the sliding table is about to disappear, making everything on it fall to the ground, Hrundi barely manages to catch the yellow telephone that is also about to tip over. And which begins to ring at precisely this moment, its ring tone mixed in with the din of the broken glass. The camera alternates first between Hrundi, who picks up the receiver—"please remain connected to the telephone," he tells the unknown person on the other end, asking in his inimitably comic, pompous manner that he not hang up, that he remain on the line—and the shots of Clutterbuck, who looks at him, holding in his hands everything he was able to save from the disaster (two glasses, as well as an ashtray). Then begins the craziest attempt at an exchange I know of, a madness that stems from how purely and simply impossible it clearly is.

What happens?

Hrundi holds the phone in his left hand and, with his right, tries to wedge the receiver between Clutterbuck's cheek and shoulder. His hand gets stuck during the transaction ("Could you just let my hand go?" he asks insistently), and then, when he manages to free it, he picks up two glasses between his fingers as the telephone cord starts to get tangled around the ashtray and the arms of the two men engaged in the exchange, each more and more incapable of completing the change in position they are trying for. It's basically a miracle that Clutterbuck can finally answer the call, that in the end he can have what is called a *phone conversation* [*échange téléphonique*], for although the vocabulary of exchange is ubiquitous in the fragments of conversation between the two busy and intertwined men ("hold," "take," "let go," they are constantly saying), their words are immediately contradicted by the inextricable interlacing of things that seems to block any possible circulation of exchange.

But most of all, what emerges from their infinite contortions is both the necessity and the impossibility of *reciprocity* in exchange. What makes us laugh here is that, instead of exchanging the telephone and glasses all at once, simultaneously, Hrundi and Clutterbuck have to engage in a whole series of relays, displacements, and delays that mean exchange properly speaking does not take place. Or rather, and more exactly, that the moment of exchange, that its singular moment, cannot be located. It is literally ungraspable (it can be neither grasped nor held onto), for it is diluted and crumbles into dust, into pulverulent micro-exchanges that look like what one might describe, to remain within the vocabulary of economics, as an infinite sequence of bridge loans or an endless chain of deposits.

Yet still more than the burlesque and its variants, there is a film genre—or rather what I would call a generic situation—in which what is at stake, the one and only thing at stake, seems to be staging the perfect reciprocity and simultaneity of exchange. I am referring to the duel in the Western, to the battle to the death that, as Alfred Hitchcock has shown masterfully, assumes as its impossible condition strict contemporaneity and pure equivalence.

Indeed, in the third episode of the first season of the series *Alfred Hitchcock Presents*, we in a sense find the generic formula of the duel as impossible exchange.[2] The episode, titled "Triggers in Leash," broadcast on October 16, 1955, consists in a duel that never takes place and that nevertheless is constantly *on the verge* of happening. The adversaries are two cowboys, Dell Delaney and Red Hillman. And the reason for their conflict—as they explain to Maggie, the manager of a small shack that serves as a country inn—is a poker game that brought them together the previous evening. Dell claims he left the game because Red, too drunk to play seriously, would have been skinned completely. Red, however, accuses Dell of having left the game after getting ahead, without giving him the chance to win back his money. Without letting him *reciprocate*, that is, *get even*.

Maggie tries to get them to listen to reason, but in vain. And this is why, as a last resort, she throws out this fateful question: "Which one is going to be the killer?" For she promises to denounce as murderer whoever shoots first, so that he is tried and hanged. Each man then waits for the other to draw first (and yet hopes to be the quicker draw); they resign themselves, settle into waiting; they sit together at the table as Maggie brings them food—she even cuts their ham, for they must *both* keep their hands visible on the table. . . . In short, time passes and the duel properly speaking still hasn't taken place even as it remains imminent.

This continues until Red has an idea: They won't draw until the hands of the clock point to exactly noon and the cuckoo comes out. "Let's begin even," Red suggests: Let's start equal or equivalent. In other words, let's wait for the signal to exchange shots *at exactly the same time, perfectly simultaneously*, so that neither of us can be accused of murder.

The camera doesn't merely alternate among shots of Red, Dell, and Maggie; it also and above all shows the clock at the precise midpoint between the two adversaries. As a result, the oscillation of its pendulum seems to literally trace the alternation—the swinging from one to the other and back—that is in the process of condensing into an *immediate reciprocity*, into the singular or stigmatic moment of the dueling exchange.

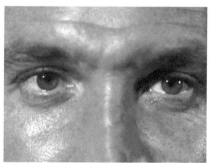

The exact hour nears, the tension mounts, becomes almost unbearable. Maggie asks the duelers, stiffened in their defiant postures, simply to let her get the crucifix on the shelves near the clock. And then we see close-ups of the antagonists' eyes, their gazes, the stakes of the duel coinciding with the filmic figure of the shot-reverse shot. Then what Maggie interprets as a sort of miracle takes place: The ticking stops, time remains suspended, as though the camera's viewpoint were stuck at the exact intersection between one gaze and the other, at the precise point of their crossing.

At this moment of arrest, the duel proves impossible; it will be deferred indefinitely, will not take place after all. But this is an infinite procrastination, an impossibility that also retains its most proper possibility: that of simultaneity and perfect reciprocity, which only take place by never happening, by remaining suspended in this waiting.

If time had not been stopped, if they had drawn at the same time, at the exact moment the cuckoo stuck its head out, in short, if the duel had taken place in and according to the perfect equality—in and according to the *equi-duality*—it seems to require, it would have tipped immediately into inequivalence, into a fateful asymmetry making one of the men, Red or Dell, the assassin of the other, Dell or Red. Transformed into a murder, the dueling exchange, in short, would have become the opposite of the exchange it was supposed to be.

It is difficult not to see in this impossible duel something like the staging of the famous, all too famous, master-slave dialectic ("lordship" and "bondage," *Herrschaft und Knechtschaft*) in the *Phenomenology of Spirit*, as though Hegel—rather than Richard Carr or Allan Vaughan Elston, listed in the credits—were the real scriptwriter behind the scenes. For what is really at stake in this ultra-famous passage in Hegel that has attracted so many interpretations and commentaries that one hardly dares reopen and reread it, I believe, is precisely the impossible *mutuality* of exchange in the recognition of one by the other.

In the *Phenomenology of Spirit* as in the duel scene in general, two "self-consciousnesses [*Selbstbewußtseine*]," as we know, "*prove* themselves and each other through a life and death struggle [*sie sich selbst und einander durch den Kampf auf Leben und Tod* bewähren]."[3] Now, this struggle to the death for recognition and self-certainty is configured, in the pages that come before this moment, as an exchange. Having posited that self-consciousness is a return from alterity or being-other [*Anderssein*] to the self, Hegel demonstrates that this alterity must itself have the structure of self-consciousness: "Self-consciousness achieves its satisfaction only in another self-consciousness [*das Selbstbewußtsein erreicht seine Befriedigung nur in einen anderen Selbstbewußtsein*]" (110), and it is only from this other that it "is recuperated" (as Hyppolite, in the vocabulary of the recuperation of debt, translates Hegel's German: *erhält sich selbst zurück*, "receives back its own self" [111]).[4] Through the other, self-consciousness "again becomes equal to itself [*es wird sich wieder gleich*]" (111), recuperates or recovers its self-equivalence. But as we know, during this process of the reappropriation of self from and through the other, the other also recovers or regains itself; it also recuperates itself as that self that it then also becomes: The self-consciousness, Hegel writes, "equally gives the other self-consciousness back again to itself [*gibt es das andere Selbstbewußtsein ihm wieder ebenso zurück*]," that is, it gives it, equally [*ebenso*], to itself (111, translation modified).

A few paragraphs later, Hegel notes that, in this reciprocal movement of the exchange of recognition between two self-consciousnesses, "we see repeated the process which presented itself as the play of Forces" (112). Now, I do not wish to, nor can I, summarize here the passage to which Hegel alludes—it is found in the preceding chapter, "Force and the Understanding"—but we must recall that what was at stake in it was change [*Wechsel*] described as absolute or pure. But when Hegel indicates that we are witnessing the repetition of the same process between two self-consciousnesses, this time it is indeed a question of exchange: *Austauschung* in German—and we aren't far from barter, *Tausch*.[5] That is why Hegel can conclude:

Each is for the other the middle term, through which each mediates itself with itself and unites with itself [*jedes ist dem Anderen die Mitte, durch welche jedes sich mit sich selbst vermittelt und zusammenschließt*]. . . . They *recognize* themselves as *mutually recognizing* themselves [*sie* anerkennen *sich als* gegenseitig sich anerkennend]. (112, translation modified)

If we could punctuate the dialectical phrase of the exchange of mutual self-recognition right here, if we could stop it before, beginning in the next paragraph, it becomes what Hegel calls the *Ungleichheit* between two parties in an exchange (Hyppolite and Bourgeois translate this as "inequality," Lefebvre as "non-parity"), we would grasp the exact instant, the precise moment, of exchange as such.

We would get a photograph or snapshot of it, so to speak. As though a photographic flash—a shot capturing one and the other, one as the other, and perhaps even one from the point of view of the other—doubled the gunshot of the duel, immobilizing it, pinning it down and anchoring it here and now, to freeze it in itself.

Indeed, the *shot*, the gunshot [*coup de feu*] that is fired, is in English also the photographic shot [*prise de vue*], what in cinema is called a frame and in photography a snapshot.

In her own way, Susan Sontag showed, in *On Photography*, that this *shot* can be at once a gunshot and a snapshot. Comparing the modern camera to a "ray gun," she sees in it a "sublimation of the gun."[6] "To photograph," she writes, "is a sublimated murder" (14–15). Or sublimated hunting:

> One situation where people are switching from bullets to film is the photographic safari that is replacing the gun safari. . . . Instead of looking through a telescopic sight to aim a rifle, they [hunters] look through a viewfinder to frame a picture.[7]

Certain Westerns have thematized brilliantly this double (or triple) sense of the word *shot*—"shooting" and "aiming" a camera (14). We can hear it, if we care to listen, in the title of John Ford's *The Man Who Shot Liberty Valance* (1962), for example: the man who killed Liberty Valance with a gunshot, of course; but also the man who filmed *Liberty Valance*, the film whose story is that of one *shot* doubling, being substituted for, or hiding behind, another, since the real lethal gunshot is not the one we thought it was. I will come back to this.

But the most literal staging of this shot that is doubled between gunshot and photographic shot is no doubt the fake final duel in *Il mio nome è nessuno* (*My Name Is Nobody*), the 1973 parody of Westerns produced and directed in part by Sergio Leone. Leone, who never hid his admiration for Ford, who even inscribes himself explicitly in Ford's lineage,[8] offers a parodic remake, so to speak, of the double shot in *The Man Who Shot Liberty Valance*.

Let's begin with the parody, then, before coming to the original.

While the two heroes, Jack Beauregard (Henry Fonda) and Nobody (Terence Hill) face each other in a New Orleans street, a photographer prepares to capture this historic settling of scores[9] in which the death of a legend (Beauregard) will mark the becoming legend of he who was . . . nobody (with or without a capital n). The outcome of the duel is awaited in a general silence; and this waiting is prolonged by the timid requests of the photographer, who has trouble framing the scene. Nobody agrees to move a bit, to allow for a "nice shot," in a sense, to be immortalized at the very moment he risks his own death. And all of a sudden, all hell breaks out: There is a double explosion, first that of the gunshot, then, as though its distant echo, that of the photographic flash as Beauregard collapses.

The percussive punctuation of the gunshot, then, is repeated in that of the photographic shot, in the snapshot of the blink of the shutter that closes, capturing the gunshot's immediate aftermath. To the extent that it registers what just took place, this photographic capture supposes as its condition of possibility the slight dissymmetry (*Ungleichheit*), that is, the lag or interval, that never fails to intrude in the moment of the exchange of gunshots, that exchange that should have been the instant of perfect simultaneity and reciprocity. But let's suppose the photographer could have taken the photograph he wanted, the photo of the very instant of the exchange rather than of its aftermath or deferred effect. What might this picture that ultimately we never see, whose possibility we only glimpse through images shown upside down, appearing backwards in the camera's viewfinder, have looked like?

Well, the photo we will never see would be the visual equivalent of the epitaph we see next: *Jack Beauregard, 1848–1899. Nobody Was Faster on the Draw*. How to understand this abyssal funerary inscription that can be read in two precisely opposite ways, as though it itself were a duel of meanings? We can of course understand it, first, as marking the victory of Nobody (of Nobody in person [*Personne en personne*], as it were): Nobody himself was quicker on the draw than Beauregard, faster than he was, and overtook him *in the blink of an eye*, exactly the time it takes for a *shot*. But second, we can also read this syntagm as a negation, as its own negation: Nobody, in the end, absolutely nobody, will have been faster than Beauregard. Between the two, it is no doubt a question, in English, of how to stress or punctuate the sentence, which thus contains within it, perfectly interchangeably (*austauschbar*, we might say, in Hegel's tongue), the two possibilities. It contains, simultaneously, oscillating from one to the other, the two possible readings, one contradicting the other and vice versa, in a sort of arrested or suspended dialectic.

The photo whose possibility we glimpse between the upside-down images, the picture the photographer was getting ready to take, although he ends up taking it only in its aftermath, this image would no doubt have, it should have, looked exactly like this phrase. On the one hand, it should have been the *image of exchange*, of exchange itself, condensed into a picture of pure reciprocity. But on the other hand, precisely because it would have shown exchange as such, it should have been itself what I will call an *exchange-image*, an image that would immediately exchange itself for its opposite. For example, it should have shown both Nobody's gaze [*regard*] and the symmetrical gaze [*regard*] of Beauregard; it should have shown them facing each other [*en regard*], face-to-face. In short, as image, it should have occupied, in the figure of a shot-reverse shot, the exact place of a hyphen or separating line.

Unless the formula has to be written by replacing the hyphen with two dots, with a sign of equivalence or reciprocal permutability, then, that would inscribe the place of the exchange-image very precisely at the limit, at the very point where the editing would cut and interchange the two halves of a line of sight between the eyes of the one and those of the other. One would then have to formulate the graph of the exchange-image as follows, with its two dots exchanging two eyes for two eyes:

Punctuating each other in the stigmatic punctiformity of an instantaneous reciprocity: This, in short, is what would be at stake in the exchange-image, in this image that does not exist but which the duel assumes or looks for without end.

If no such image exists, it is for a reason we started to glimpse through Deleuze, a reason that is really quite simple but whose consequences are abyssal: *There is no exchange; there is only credit or debt.* To put this differently, and formalized to the extreme, no doubt: Once time is introduced into the exchange, once exchange takes time—as it always does—it becomes impossible to distinguish rigorously between exchange and credit or debt. For an exchange that is not simultaneous would place one of the two parties in the exchange in the position of debtor and the other in the position of creditor, if only for a time, no matter how brief, how short.

I cannot enter here into the philosophical genealogy of such a notion, which would make debt the occulted ground of exchange. One would have to trace it, as Deleuze and Guattari suggest in *Anti-Oedipus*, at least to the Nietzsche of *On the Genealogy of Morality*, which appeared in 1887; or perhaps even, already, to a fragment on equity published in 1880 in *Human, All Too Human*.[10] What interests me are the philosophical stakes of debt in terms of the economics of the image, what I call the iconomy of the visible.

To try to outline this, allow me to turn to the other Western I already alluded to: *The Man Who Shot Liberty Valance*, whose protagonist is named Ransom and in whose title is inscribed the issue of value or valuation.

The narrative structure of the film is that of a flashback. Senator Ransom Stoddard (James Stewart) returns to the little town of Shinbone with his wife (Vera Miles) to attend the funeral of Tom Doniphon (John Wayne). During an interview with the local newspaper, he tells how, decades earlier, the stagecoach he was traveling in was attacked by a band of robbers led by the outlaw Liberty Valance (Lee Marvin). Nearly beaten to death, Ransom is helped by Doniphon and then taken care of by the owner of a restaurant and his wife (he will marry their daughter Hallie).

Later, as Ransom is waiting on tables at his protectors' restaurant, Valance tries to humiliate him and Doniphon comes to his defense. A latent war sets in between the future senator and the outlaw. It doesn't take long for it to break out: When Ransom is elected to represent the city at the territory's convention, Valance talks him into a duel.

Let's consider this—yet another!—duel. For rather than a challenge worthy of the name, this is an anti-duel, a non-duel that, far from being a quest for recognition between equals in a battle to the death, is more like a methodical exercise in which one humiliates the other. Valance first wounds Ransom's arm. He then allows him to pick his gun back up and promises, "This time right between the eyes." And this is where the dramatic turn of events that gives the film its name takes place: Although nobody expects it, Ransom, known as slow on the draw par excellence, the clumsiest person with a gun[11]—with a well-aimed shot, Ransom becomes "the man who shot Liberty Valance." He becomes the hero.

In this anti-duel, as in those supposedly authentic duels we have seen previously, once again the exchange of gazes is at least as important as the gunshots. But the apparent visual reciprocity of the shot-reverse shot, this time, gives way to the dissymmetry between shadow and light, between withdrawal [*retrait*] and visibility. "Come closer, where I can see you," Liberty has to tell Ransom. "Get out of that shadow, dude." The inequality, the *Ungleichheit*, Hegel speaks of is obvious everywhere, from the difference in skill between the two duelers to the left-right inequivalence that becomes clear when Ransom, picking up his gun in his only good arm, hears Liberty tell him, "You've got two hands, pick it up."

However, as we will learn later, the exchange will in a sense have been perfect; there will indeed have been a perfectly instantaneous substitution of one shot for another. But hidden. Yet an exchange that remains hidden, unknown to the parties in the exchange, is no doubt not worthy of the name. The condition of mutuality, the symmetry and simultaneity of recognition, as well as reciprocity in visibility, is lacking.

What is this hidden exchange? And what happened?

After becoming "the man who shot Liberty Valance," Ransom goes to the convention to run in the election for members of Congress. And there he hears that it would be unjust to elect a man merely because he killed someone. His own reputation becomes an embarrassment. Doniphon, in an ultimate act of sacrificial generosity, then admits that it was really he who shot Liberty in the duel (a duel that thus expands into a secret triangulation), that he drew at the same time as Ransom, simultaneously, exchanging from the shadows that hid him one shot and one vigilante for the other, in an absolute coincidence.

A second flashback then begins, one flashback within the other, when the camera closes in on Doniphon's eyes. The smoke from his cigarette acts as a fade-out and takes us into the past, to the repetition of the scene of the duel, this time filmed from a different point of view.

Thanks to the perfect but secret exchange that traverses it, the duel that was never one, this anti-duel, in whatever sense one takes it, becomes an image of infinite debt, of absolute dissymmetry: One person, Ransom, is infinitely in debt, is indebted to the death of the other, Liberty, for what becomes his glory, his reputation; but he is also and above all the debtor of the other other, Doniphon, who embodies a sort of bridge loan, as it were, an intermediary and supplemental debt that allows him to take out the principal debt to which he owes his fame.

It thus turns out that the perfect exchange shelters within it an abyssal and perfectly asymmetrical debt (a debt that even verges on having been entered into without the debtor's knowledge). It hides a sort of ransom that Ransom carries inscribed in his name—while Liberty, in the end, dies free; he will have been *worth* his freedom, but according to a valuation that is also absolutely dissymmetrical, since it is precisely that of death (after all, as Hegel says, life itself is "as essential [*so wesentlich*]" to self-consciousness as its negation in the freedom that chooses death).[12]

Across this network of debts that frame the film, in the gap—no matter how tiny or instantaneous—that opens every debit account, Ford's Western in its own way says that *the image takes time and thus money.* The image, in other words, is always on credit. We are still and always very close to what Deleuze suggested in the iconomic formulations we have already auscultated (in fact, despite appearances we have never lost sight of them). For the images that will have been taken thus—yes, *shot*, during the shooting of the fake duel scene in *The Man Who Shot Liberty Valance*—these images look forward to others that, much later, in a flashback enveloped in a flashback, will give or return their value to them. One could go so far as to say, taking up a line from one of Antonioni's characters somewhat provocatively, that *there are no images*, in the sense of this iconomic law according to which an image is always more or less than an image: It is not yet the

▷ *Photo Gallery: Blow-Up, or Why There Are No Images.*

image it will be, but it will be the image it is only on the condition of passing the baton to another, on the condition of already no longer being the image it is. An image has value only in relation to other images, as Bresson put it so well and so simply for his poetics of the cinematographer.

But the question that awaits us, then, as we recall, is this: Must we limit Bresson's and Deleuze's statements to cinema *stricto sensu* or can we extend their meaning to the general iconomy of a metacinema that is synonymous with the world? I will return to this in the final lecture.

But I would like to emphasize once again that the properly iconomic stakes are not only possible images of debt. It is not simply a matter of images that might represent and make visible the indebtedness of this or that character (of Ransom to Doniphon, for example), but rather of this: How might an image, as such, always be indebted to other images? This is what I will attempt to think by rereading some of Walter Benjamin's texts: In the circulation and exchange of images that weave the texture [*trame*] of our gaze and put it into motion—that *innervate* it, as we will see, more than ever today—there are only debt-images or credit-images.[13]

In anticipation of, or as the trailer for, what we will consider in the third lecture, then, I would like to mention, finally, an episode from another television series I am fond of.

Why a TV series, yet another one, you will ask, after *The Sopranos* in the first lecture and Hitchcock's duel in this lecture? Because TV, because the seriality of televisual temporality, anticipates precisely the generalization of debt, from cinema to metacinema, from the restricted iconomy of film to the general iconomy of the visible. As Rudolf Arnheim writes in a visionary article (despite its sometimes apocalyptic tone):

> Television will replace bodily presence [*die leibliche Gegenwart*] still better than radio did, and it will thus further deepen the ditch around the island onto which the individual withdraws. And the spiritual commercial balance of this island will become all the more passive [*und die geistige Handelsbilanz dieser Insel wird umso passiver werden*]: valuables [*Kostbarkeiten*] will be imported from the world over, consumption with no production in return [*Konsum ohne Gegenleistung*].[14]

If cinema, as we will see, is already a construction that produces the indebted gaze, television and TV series perhaps complete the process, making this debt infinite. On the so-called small screen, the iconomic stakes of the debt-image extend beyond cinema, taking over other screens and gradually investing seeing itself, with the naked eye and without any apparent screen, in the arche-film of the world.[15]

I would like to conclude by recalling an episode that is part of the second season of *The Twilight Zone.* Titled "A Most Unusual Camera," it aired on December 16, 1960. We witness the strange and tragic adventure of Chester and Paula Diedrich, a couple that makes its living from burglary. Among the objects in their latest spoils is an old, worthless camera. On its case, which cannot be opened, is written, in a "crazy foreign writing," the following inscription, in French: "Dix à la propriétaire" ("Ten to the owner"). Its meaning will be made clear later: Every owner of this strange cube will only be able to take ten photos, each picture the image of what will happen to them five minutes later. After a moment of amazement and fear, the three robbers (Paula's brother has joined them in the meantime) wonder how to make use of this singular machine. They can do nothing with it, they at first think; there's nothing to be gained from it. Chester then for a moment considers making it a gift to humanity—just like that, for nothing, as a pure, disinterested gift. But seeing the horse races on television, Chester hits upon on the idea that, thanks to the camera, they will be able to win every bet they place. Very quickly, however, their winnings give way to the worst case scenario: The future captured by the camera is none other than that of the instant of the death of each of the three characters—and even of a fourth: The hotel valet who will try to steal this *peau de chagrin* in the guise of a roll of film.

What is remarkable about this episode is that it makes visible what is inscribed in the temporality of the image, that is, the promise of its return—the same image, five minutes later. And this promised recurrence is immediately translated in terms of profitability, of return on investment: When the image comes back, it carries a profit; the bet (on the horses, for example) will have been won. It is as though the time of the image here became an unceasing advance, a time on credit. But this is a credit that in the end comes down to a single payment in the form of an arche-debt: For the return anticipated, one pays with one's life.

"A Most Unusual Camera" thus becomes the allegory par excellence of the iconomy of debt: A shot is the image that it is only by being immediately deferred in its impossible return to itself, in its impossible self-equivalence. Put differently, between the image and its self-coincidence the delay of a postponement or gap opens, of a debt that can be made good only in death.

THREE

Innervation, or The Gaze of Capital

In the first lecture, on Monday, I left a question hanging. Cinema, I said with Deleuze and a few others, is more than cinema: It is the name of the world. And I concluded, at least as a hypothesis, that filmic iconomy would have to be generalized into a supermarket of the visible that exceeds the borders of cinema. In other words, Deleuze's metacinema—what I would call the archefilmic structure of the world—corresponds to the general iconomy of a hypermarket. In still other words, the folded structure of what I analyzed, at the end of the *Sopranos* episode, as the gaze *of* money (in the double sense of an objective and subjective genitive) might well be that of sight *tout court*.

I sketched this movement toward a general iconomy again in the second lecture, on Wednesday, before considering some images from another series, *The Twilight Zone*. And again, I left this movement hanging, though not without suggesting in passing that with television the iconomic stakes begin to exceed cinema, invading all sorts of other screens, perhaps even entering into visibility as such. Deleuze said nothing else, really, when he took up Serge Daney's idea of a "stage" or "state" of the image that, under the name of television, transforms the whole world into cinema: "The world itself 'turns into film'; any film at all, and this is what television amounts to, when the world is turning into any film at all."[1]

What Deleuze suggests, however, only makes my question more pointed. How can one assert, on the one hand, that the world *is* cinema and, on the other, that at a certain stage or in a certain state of its becoming it *is turning into* cinema? (How does one go from the world *as* cinema to the world *becoming* cinema?) Moreover, is it not that the world is or is becoming cinema even beyond television, beyond the screens the world is covered with, in the very texture of its visibility? Which, to me, amounts once again to asking: Are we witnessing a growing commodification of seeing or are we seeing the arche-iconomic texture of the visible shine through like never before? This is the aporetic knot that I am not sure this third and final lecture will ultimately succeed in freeing itself from: the supermarket of the visible, always already, but always more.

To try to think this generalization of the iconomy of which cinema and then television are the name or announcement, the path I will follow begins with Walter Benjamin (although we will also cross paths with Deleuze—him again!—somewhere along the road). It will lead us from Benjamin's concepts of medium and innervation to an archaeology of what we will have to call the *paths of the gaze* [*voies du regard*], precisely, that is, the *road networks of the visible* [*voiries du visible*], all the ways in which sight can be mobilized, channeled, tracked along the rails[2] of a universal iconomic circulation. We will thus witness the planetary deployment of the actual transportation infrastructure of visibility (elevators and escalators, for example) that make possible its market iconomy. And we will then see these infrastructures become absorbed, incorporated, thanks to film, in a gaze that is henceforth *innervated* by the market that constitutes its medium.[3]

This gaze is ours. It is the gaze of the *high-speed debtor-downloaders* [*très hauts débiteurs*] *of images* that we have become.

▷ *Locations*: 23, rue Bénard, Paris 14th

Let's begin, then, with Benjamin and a preliminary problem that could be formulated as follows: How does a medium become immediate? How, that is, according to a logic that is as paradoxical as it is rigorous (this, essentially, is the very logic of the concept of medium), how is a medium *immediated* to become the medium that it is? In still other words, how is a medium thinned out or spirited away, becoming immediately active while disappearing?

Benjamin poses this problem explicitly in a posthumous fragment that was probably written around 1920. I will read it as literally as possible in order better to auscultate all its resonances:

> The medium [*das Medium*] through which works of art act [*wirken*] on subsequent eras is always different from the one through which they acted on their own era; and in these subsequent eras it continues to change constantly in relation to ancient works [*es wechselt auch in jenen spätern Zeiten den alten Werken gegenüber immer wieder*]. But this medium is always thinner [clearer, lighter, or finer, even more liquid: *dünner*], relatively speaking, than the one through which, at the time of their birth, these works acted on their contemporaries. . . . For the creator [*Schöpfer*], the medium is so dense [so thick: *so dicht*] around his work that he no doubt cannot cross [pierce or penetrate: *durchdringen*] it by relating to the approach [or position: *Einstellung*] that the work asks of people; he can do this only through the detour of an indirect relation, so to speak. The composer would perhaps see his music, the painter hear his painting, the poet feel [*abtasten*] his poem if he tried to get very close to it.[4]

What happens to the concept of medium here?

First and foremost, a medium, Benjamin says, is not given as such, invariably or immutably: If medium is that through which the work or more generally the sensible artifact passes in order to be perceived—if it is what they must penetrate or pierce—this passage is like the clearing of a path in a milieu, in an element of *varying density*, more or less thick or fluid. In other texts we will have to read closely, Benjamin names this clearing *innervation*. The fact remains that the becoming-medium of the medium—that is, paradoxically, its becoming-transparent or immediate, its immediation—thus takes time.

Moreover, the medium seems to be able to become the medium it is—with a capacity for immediate transduction, which is precisely what allows passage to take place—only if it is first relayed by another medium: Before being an immediate medium, the visibility of the painter can first be traversed only by passing through the audibility of the musician, or vice versa. And as for the poet, he must touch his writing. In short, if it is true that the very concept of medium necessarily contains within it the idea of a certain transparency (things must circulate throughout a medium, which is to say that the medium becomes a medium only by effacing itself to a certain extent), then what Benjamin's fragment suggests is that medium only becomes translucent by thickening itself, necessarily, through its reference to another medium. The becoming-medium of medium demands its multiplication into media.

But a closer look at the list of the detours from one medium to another that is sketched out here shows that tactility is not merely a supplementary example of deviation added to the others. If the visible or the audible can be crossed in the first place only by passing through one another, the passage of poetic language—and even of language in general, which Benjamin also thinks as a medium[5]—through tactile palpation is on a different level. Touching, insofar as it implies direct transduction rather than translation, indeed seems to be the paradigm of the becoming-medium of every medium as a propagation at a distance *by contact*: Are the qualities of density and thickness—or, on the contrary, of thinness, fineness, even liquidity—not in the end haptic categories?

In short, if it is true, as Benjamin suggests, that becoming-medium first necessarily passes through the detour of another medium, the detour through the tactile would name the very mediumness of medium as such. Which, however, should not lead us to posit a pure mediumness of touching, as though touching, because it is absolutely immediate, were an absolute medium. Rather, this should lead us to think that touching has the quality of a medium only because it is the element or milieu par excellence of self-difference, of the distance to oneself in which the technological prosthesis is already woven.[6]

Benjamin's singular notion of innervation at first names this tactility of medium a *putting into contact*.

What, then, is innervation for Benjamin? And how does this concept allow us to understand better the becoming-medium of every medium, that is, how the immediation that constitutes it as medium is opened up in it?

The word *Innervation* makes its appearance in Benjamin's writings beginning in 1927. We come across it in a passage from *One-Way Street [Einbahnstraße]* that seems to echo the concluding remark from the 1920 fragment on the poet feeling his poem:

> The typewriter will alienate the hand of the man of letters from the pen only when the precision of typographic forms [*die Genauigkeit typographischer Formungen*] has directly entered the conception of his books. One might suppose that new systems with more variable typefaces [*Schriftgestaltung*] would then be needed. They will replace the pliancy of the hand [*der geläufigen Hand*] with the innervation of commanding fingers [*die Innervation der befehlenden Finger*].[7]

It is tempting indeed to read this aphorism in terms of the resonances of what Benjamin said about the poet in 1920: that the medium of poetic language became transparent or translucid for him—became medium, then—only thanks to a detour through touching. Digital innervation seems to play a similar role here: Through it typography and literary conception will be (im)mediately *in contact.*

We can come to a first understanding of innervation in Benjamin by following this tactile and manual motif. Let's stay close to the hand and its fingers, then: no longer those of the poet or man of letters, but this time those of the gambler. In a posthumous fragment from 1929–30 titled "Notes on a Theory of Gambling [*Notizen zu einer Theorie des Spiels*]," Benjamin writes:

> Certain matters are clear. What is decisive is the level of motor innervation [*die motorische Innervation*], and the more emancipated it is from optical perception [*je mehr sie von der optischen Wahrnehmung emanzipiert ist*], the more decisive it is. From this stems a principal commandment for gamblers: they must use their hands sparingly, in order to respond to the slightest innervations [*um sie den leisesten Innervationen gefügig zu Machen*]. The gambler's basic approach [*Grundverfassung*] must, so to speak, adumbrate the subtlest network of inhibitions [*ein feinstes Geflecht von Hemmungen darstellen*], which lets only the most minute and unassuming innervations pass through its meshes [*die nur die allerunscheinbarsten, geringfügigsten Innervationen durch ihre Maschen hindurchlassen*].[8]

These lines bear the traces of the vocabulary of Freudian psychoanaly-sis, from which Benjamin's notion of innervation is very likely borrowed (I will return to this). The inhibitions in question seem to produce a filtering that is also a freeing, an unbinding, of motor function with respect to visual, that is, here, conscious, perception. For innervation to open up or allow for passage, consciousness must have been inhibited, short-circuited in favor of the unconscious.[9] What follows in the fragment confirms this very clearly by opposing the experienced gambler to the ill-informed one; for what the gamblers do or do not have knowledge of is precisely the role of the unconscious in the game, insofar as the unconscious *does not want to know anything about knowledge* [*ne veut rien savoir du savoir*]:

> When a winning number is clearly predicted but not bet on, the man who is not in the know will conclude that he is in excellent form and that next time he just needs to act more promptly, more boldly. Whereas anyone familiar with the game will know that a single incident of this kind is sufficient to tell him that he must break off instantly. For it is a sign that the contact between his motor innervation and "fate" has been interrupted [*der Kontakt der motorischen Innervation mit dem "Schicksal" gelöst ist*]. Only then will "what is to come [*das 'Kommende'*]" enter his consciousness more or less clearly as what it is.—Also established is the fact that no one has so many chances of betting on a winning number as someone who has just made a significant win. This means that the correct sequence is based not on any previous knowledge of the future but on a correct physical predisposition, which is increased in immediacy, certainty, and uninhibitedness by every confirmation, such as is provided by a win [*die durch jede Bestätigung, wie ein Gewinn sie darstellt, in ihrer Unmittelbarkeit, Sicherheit, Hemmungslosigkeit gesteigert wird*].[10]

It is by short-circuiting consciousness that motor innervation thus clears a path: It reinforces itself, it gains in immediacy, with each passage throughout the winning sequence. It tends to crystallize into a conductive medium that allows for *more and more passage* between the player and the game. In short, each time, more and more each time, innervation conducts or transmits a sort of electrical discharge—"lightning quick innervation at the moment of danger [*die blitzschnelle Innervation in der Gefahr*]" (298, translation modified), Benjamin notes at the end of the same fragment—a discharge that *consolidates the immediate fluidity*, as it were, paradoxically, of innervating conduction.

As in the 1920 fragment, we also witness here the *immediation of the becoming-medium*.

Before I continue with my reading of the passages in which Benjamin's concept of innervation clears its passage, I should no doubt consider briefly the likely source of the word in Freud.[11]

Innervation plays a major role in Freud's early writings and especially in his *Studies on Hysteria*, which he wrote with Breuer in 1895. Indeed, hysteria is described and analyzed as "the repression [*Verdrängung*] of an incompatible idea" that, however, persists "as a memory trace that is weak (has little intensity)," while the "affect that is torn from it would be used for a somatic innervation [*Innervation*]"; that is, "the excitation is converted [*Konversion*]."[12] The notion of innervation is also present in one of Freud's works that we know Benjamin read, *Jokes and Their Relation to the Unconscious*, which appeared in 1905.[13] There, innervation is thought in terms of anticipation, as the hand preparing for what comes; speaking of what "we are used to anticipating with our representations," Freud writes:

> If I am expecting to catch a ball which is being thrown at me, I put my body in states of tension [*versetze ich meinen Körper in Spannungen*] in order to enable me to withstand the collision with the ball, and the superfluous motions [*die überschüssigen Bewegungen*] which I make if the ball turns out to be light make me look comical to the spectators. . . . A similar thing happens if, for example, I lift out a basket of fruit which I took to be heavy but which was hollow and formed out of wax in order to deceive me. By its upward jerk my arm betrays that I have prepared a superfluous innervation for its purpose [*eine für den Zweck übergroße Innervation vorbereitet hatte*] and hence I am laughed at. (79–80)

The unconscious, the preparation of the hand or body tensed in anticipation of what comes: These are the principal traits of Benjamin's concept of innervation as it crystallizes in the course of the writings from the end of the 1920s and the beginning of the 1930s. The only thing missing, no doubt, is another motif—electricity—which also appears diffusely but insistently in Freud's corpus, beginning in 1894 with *The Neuro-Psychoses of Defense*.[14] For innervation, which had the quality of a flash of lightning in the notes on gambling, will be explicitly *electrified* when Benjamin, in his

1931 homage to Paul Valéry, cites a passage from Valéry on electrical current as the "general innervation of the world."[15]

A question persists, however, when we follow the path cleared by innervation from Freud's work to Benjamin's writings. In Freud, innervation is most often described as a sort of already constituted road network of nerves that psychic excitation can take or not on its route to the bodily or sensorial extremities, as though it were located at the intersection of several possible paths that have already been traced; but it also appears in certain passages as the force of clearing that *opens* pathways, as the *road network management* [*agent voyer*] itself. Thus, between "A Case of Successful Treatment by Hypnotism" and, two years later, the *Studies on Hysteria*, Freud seems to hesitate: In 1892–93, he considers the painful ideas of the hysteric to "have found the path to bodily innervation [*den Weg zur Körperinnervation fanden*]," as though this path were available to these ideas; then, in the 1895 text, while analyzing the case of Emmy von N., he speaks of the "process of innervation itself [*der Innervationsvorgang selbst*]."[16]

As we began to see when reading the notes on the hand of the winning gambler (the gambler who wins more and more by strengthening, confirming, the winning innervation), it is this second conception that Benjamin adopts. And that is why innervation, in Benjamin, is never a vehicular network that is already there to be followed, but the *opening of a path for a routing*—if we understand this opening in the most active sense, as consonant with *tracing*—that feels its way toward what comes. It is a medium *on the way* to its immediation.

Little by little, then, the notion of innervation branches out and forms paths in Benjamin's work: *Innervation innervates the corpus* of his writings, outlining the contours of another thinking of medium.

Let's continue to follow its paths in order to get a sense of their most explicitly political stakes.

At the end of 1928 or the beginning of 1929, Benjamin wrote for his friend Asja Lacis the "Program for a Proletarian Children's Theatre [*Programm eines proletarischen Kindertheaters*]," which remained in manuscript form. Having described the painter as "a man who sees more accurately with his hand when his eye fails him, who is able to transfer the receptive innervation of the ocular muscles [*die aufnehmende Innervation der Sehmuskeln*] to the creative innervation [*die schöpferische Innervation*] of the hand," Benjamin indicates concisely that, in the same way, "every child's gesture is . . . [a] creative innervation" that "is exactly proportioned to the receptive innervation."[17] Now, as the title of this manifesto clearly indicates, as do the "Prefatory Remarks" that open it, what is at stake is the role of infancy in the "proletarian movement." "Catchphrases," Benjamin declares (or slogans: *Phrasen* is often pejorative in German), "have no power at all [*gar keine Gewalt*] over children": "The party program is no instrument of a class-conscious education, because the element of ideology, important though it is, reaches the child only as a catchphrase [*als Phrase*]."[18] As in the case of the gambler's hand, it is a question—let's continue to extend the electrical metaphor that comes to us from Freud—of *short-circuiting* consciousness, conscious discourse.[19]

Benjamin theorizes this politics of short-circuiting in an important article on surrealism he published in the review *Die literarische Welt* in February 1929. This is a politics *of* the unconscious in the double sense of the (objective and subjective) genitive: a politics that at once has the unconscious as its object (that would be *about* the unconscious and its place in politics) and whose subject is the unconscious (that is decided in and by the unconscious).

The short-circuit takes place, literally, in the final three pages of the article, which introduces a concept—the "image-space [*Bildraum*]"—that will prove inseparable from that of innervation.[20] Introducing a distinction between comparison or metaphor and image (that is, if we prefer, between the *mediate* and the *immediate* image), Benjamin writes: "Nowhere do these two—metaphor and image—collide so drastically and so irreconcilably as in politics" (56). As in the pedagogy of proletarian theater, one must therefore "expel moral metaphor from politics" (56), that is, exclude metaphoric or discursive mediation, in order, on the contrary, "to discover in the sphere of political action a one hundred per cent image-space" [*im Raum des politischen Handelns den hundertprozentigen Bildraum entdecken*] (56, translation modified). And this "image-space," Benjamin immediately specifies, "can no longer be measured out by contemplation" (56). At stake, in the end, is a rupture with the bourgeois notion of art or of the artistic work in favor of a sort of absolute performativity in the political effect of the aesthetic (but far, as far as possible, from any idea of a proletarian art, which would change nothing):

> In reality it is far less a matter of making the artist of bourgeois origin into a master of "proletarian art" than of deploying him, even at the expense of his artistic activity, at important points in this image-space [*an wichtigen Orten dieses Bildraums*]. Indeed, might not perhaps the interruption of his "artistic career" be an essential part of his new function?
>
> The jokes [*Witze*] he tells are the better for it. And he tells them better. For in the joke, too, in invective, in misunderstanding [*auch im Witz, in der Beschimpfung, im Mißverständnis*], in all cases where an action puts forth its own image and is its own image [*überall, wo ein Handeln selber das Bild aus sich herausstellt und ist*], . . . where nearness looks at itself with its own eyes [*wo die Nähe sich selbst aus den Augen sieht*], the image-space we are seeking opens up, the world of universal and integral actuality [*die Welt allseitiger und integraler Aktualität*]. (56, translation modified)

This space of the direct action of images—where images act directly— obeys the unconscious logic of the *Witz* and the *lapsus*.[21] As Benjamin puts it, in one of those striking formulations he has a knack for: In the space where images are nearly called upon to *touch one another* (to collide with, rub up against, or propagate one another, immediately and without any distance), it is proximity itself, it is nearness as such, that *looks at itself*, eye to eye. Which amounts to saying that what Benjamin imagines here—what he dreams of, whether his eyes are open or closed—is a visibility without gap: a visibility so full and performative that it would short-circuit every re-presentation, becoming confused with the blinding flash or *Blitz* of the invisible and unforeseeable event.

In what we might henceforth call a *visibility of contact*, where, then, has innervation, the mediality or mediumness of medium, gone? Has it been fulfilled, that is, reduced to an immediate and total conduction?

Let's wait a bit before responding.

For if we blink here we'll start to see a strange and improbable, a no doubt unheard of and anachronistic, encounter—between Benjamin and Deleuze.

To be sure, not only does Deleuze almost never cite Benjamin, not only is Benjamin not among the constellation of authors who accompany Deleuze on the path of his thinking, but one finds, here and there, Deleuzian statements that, while they do not explicitly mention Benjamin, clearly seem to want to mark a distance from him.[22] Yet despite everything that seems to keep them at a distance, Deleuze and Benjamin cross paths or brush up against each other most when they both try, a half century apart, to think the world as integrally composed of images, as woven or constituted by images that are not representations of this world so much as they are its very matter, its movement, and its becoming. Deleuze thus speaks of an "infinite whole of all images" that "constitutes a kind of plane of immanence"—that is, that has no outside, that *is* its own outside. And he adds that "this in-itself of the image is matter: not something hidden behind the image, but on the contrary the absolute identity of the image and movement" (*Movement-Image*, 58–59). Is this not a striking echo of the *Bildraum*, of the "one hundred per cent image-space" that Benjamin spoke of in 1929? As strange as it is, the silent proximity of the two thinkers is undeniable. And it stems, of course, from their common source, in these pages, Henri Bergson's *Matter and Memory*.[23]

In short, in the encounter without encounter between Deleuze and Benjamin, it is a matter of the *contact* of images, with and between themselves. And that is why, moreover, both no doubt take us to the limits of the concept of the image itself: where the space of images *is brimming over with plenitude*, where the reduction, the resorption of the gap that allows for and constitutes an image as such, dissolves the image, so to speak, in its pure and immediate performativity as image.

Within the integral actuality of the *Bildraum*, one hundred percent full of images that touch and act directly upon one another, there is in Benjamin, however, a sort of interstitial residue that is none other than its very innervation. Indeed, in the final page of the article on surrealism, at its close, the word appears again, naming in a sense *what remains* of the bodily or material mediation (of medium) within the purest immediation: "A remainder remains" [*es bleibt ein Rest*], Benjamin writes. And he continues:

> The collective is a body too [*auch das Kollektivum ist leibhaft*]. And the *physis*
> that is being organized for it in technology can, through all its political and

factual reality, only be produced in that image-space [*in jenem Bildraume*]. . . .
Only when in technology body and image space so interpenetrate [*sich Leib und
Bildraum so tief durchdringen*] that all revolutionary tension [*Spannung*] becomes
bodily collective innervation [*leibliche kollektive Innervation*], and all the bodily
innervations of the collective become revolutionary discharge [*Entladung*], has
reality transcended itself to the extent [*hat die Wirklichkeit so sehr sich selbst über-
troffen*] demanded by the *Communist Manifesto*. (56, translation modified)

What remains—between images and images, between images and image-
bodies—is thus the innervating clearing that weaves this space of images in
the immediacy of its activity. What remains between is also (im)mediately
what abolishes the between. Or vice versa.

But since this is the path on which the concept of innervation henceforth
undertakes its clearing, we must now go in the direction of Marx. Where,
in a new anachronism, it too fulminating and fast as lightning, we will once
again find Deleuze.

How we perceive—see, hear, touch, sense in general—is the historical product of economic and social relations: Marx states this very early and utterly
explicitly in his *1844 Manuscript*, when he writes that the five senses are
constructed and that their construction is the "labour of the entire history
of the world down to the present."[24] And we find the echo of this historicity
of sensible perception (of *aisthēsis*) in Benjamin from the first version of his
essay "The Work of Art in the Age of Its Technological Reproducibility" in
1935; for him it is a question, precisely, of medium (we will return to this):
"The way in which human perception is organized [*die menschliche Wahrne-
hmung sich organisiert*]—the medium [*Medium*] in which it occurs—is conditioned [*bedingt*] not only by nature but by history" (23).[25]

At about the same time, in the "Notes and Materials" he assembled for
his *Arcades Project*, Benjamin recopied these exact lines from Marx on the
"social organs," the same lines I quoted in the first lecture. And, filing
them, appropriately, in the *Konvolut* titled *Marx*, he prefaced them with the
following note: "On the Doctrine of Revolutions as Innervations of the
Collective."[26] What he adds to the definitions of the concept of innervation
he has already gathered together, then, is the idea that a socially shared
perceptual prosthesis comes to life and to consist organically in order to

sense. This idea was sketched out in the manifesto of proletarian theater for children and in the article on surrealism. It then crystallizes in Benjamin's text around Marx's name.

Benjamin undertakes the analysis of this equipment of *aisthēsis*—of what we might describe, in a sense I have attempted to point to elsewhere, as a *general organology of the sensible*[27]—in the different versions of "The Work of Art in the Age of Its Technological Reproducibility." . . . And it is there, then, that the ultimate meanings and resonances of the concept of innervation unfold. We must now auscultate them in detail, for they will lead us toward what I have begun to call, as a hypothesis, the supermarket of the visible.

In the first German version of the essay, in 1935, the word *Innervation* appears only once, when Benjamin describes an "emancipated technology" of which man is "no longer the master" and which nevertheless becomes for him "like a second nature":

> Film serves to train men in those new apperceptions and reactions [*in denjenigen neuen Apperzeptionen und Reaktionen zu üben*] that condition the use of equipment [*Apparatur*] whose role in their life increases almost every day. To make the monstrous technical equipment of our time the object of human innervation [*die ungeheure technische Apparatur unserer Zeit zum Gegenstande der menschlichen Innervation zu machen*] is the historical task in whose service film finds its true meaning.[28]

Cinema is thus a way of training (*üben*) oneself, of becoming accustomed to a technological mechanism. Of making it second nature, that is, of incorporating it like an artificial graft that becomes organic, that ends up becoming part of what is supposed to be the body proper, like its innervated flesh.

In Pierre Klossowski's 1936 French translation, which was overseen by Benjamin, the same passage is taken up and developed in a long note, whose beginning, at least, we must read in the context of what leads up to it:

> *Film serves to train man in the apperception and reaction determined by the use of a technical equipment whose role in his life constantly increases in importance.* This role will teach him that his momentary enslavement to this set of tools will only give way to freeing by this same set of tools when the economic structure of

humanity has been adapted to the new productive forces put in motion by the second technology.*

*The very goal of revolutions is to accelerate this adaptation. Revolutions are the innervations of the collective element or, more exactly, the attempts at the innervation of the collectivity that for the first time finds its organs in the second technology.[29]

The Marxian origin of the motif of organic innervation, as it appears explicitly in the Konvolut from *The Arcades Project* that I have already quoted, remains implicit here even as it is clearly perceptible. But there are also other more or less audible echoes of Marx in the text that we must listen to in order to try to understand what we are incorporating by innervating the filmic mechanism. For it is clear that, with what Benjamin calls the "second technology" (to which we are coming), it is not simply a question of seeing better or more or differently. At stake in its incorporation is not only the increased acuity of the gaze, its power as visual surgery, or its penetrating endoscopy as these are evoked a bit later.[30] What the organological graft of the filmic mechanism transplants and imports into us is a gaze that, as it becomes sharper, itself also becomes a market of exchanges, that is, the field or theater of the fictions of exchange.

What is this "second technology" whose effects and consequences Benjamin explores? His thesis is well known, but it is worth recalling. This technology, which he characterizes as "mechanical," is described as "second" in contrast to a "first" one that, as in "prehistoric art," is "still confused with ritual" ("L'Oeuvre d'art," 716). But most of all, the two technologies diverge with regard to the space they maintain for reproducibility. As Benjamin writes in the final version of his essay in 1938: "*The unique value* [der einzigartige Wert] *of the 'authentic' work of art has its basis in ritual, the source of its original use value* [Gebrauchswert]" (Benjamin's emphasis).[31] Yet this value, which Benjamin also names "cult value [*Kultwert*]," this use value in the cult or rites, is opposed to what Benjamin calls "exhibition value [*Ausstellungswert*]." Which it is difficult not to interpret, then, as an *exchange value* in the Marxian sense: Marx's famous conceptual couple—*Gebrauchswert* and *Tauschwert*, use value and exchange value—is translated here into the specific terms of an economy of images, an iconomy.

In the long perspective he takes and that leads from parietal art to cinema, Benjamin wants to understand how this iconomy of the value of images acts on aesthetics understood in the Greek sense of a "theory of perception."[32] Still more precisely, what he pursues are the iconomic determinations of the gaze. For on the one hand, the hypothetical or asymptotic limit of a pure use value of the image is that it not be seen. And on the other, the limit of its pure exchange value is its dissolution in the infinity of gazes to which it is exposed.[33]

According to Benjamin, the current iconomy tends precisely toward this second limit, that of pure exchange value: "Today," he writes in the first version of 1935, "the absolute emphasis placed on the exhibition value [of the work of art] assigns it entirely new functions, among which the one we are conscious of—the 'artistic' function—subsequently appears rudimentary."[34] The images that circulate for and before our eyes would thus have almost no other consistency than that of their ability to pass from gaze to gaze.

But this metamorphosis of iconicity also corresponds to a mutation of the gaze directed toward it. It becomes scattered or dispersed, Benjamin says: *Zerstreut*, he writes in German, that is, in the 1936 French version, "distrait," "distracted" (736). We have to understand this word literally, possibly inserting a hyphen between the prefix (*dis-*) and the root (which comes from the Latin *tractus*, from *trahere*: "to pull"). With that hyphen what the signifier says is remarked in the signifier itself: To be *dis-trait*, dis-tracted, is to be carried away by a trait, by a traction that pulls or attracts elsewhere.

Benjamin finds the model of this dis-tracted vision in the perception of architecture, which, he says, introduces into optics an anoptic, that is, tactile, element:[35]

> Buildings are received in a twofold manner: . . . tactilely and optically. Such reception cannot be understood precisely by thinking of the gathering of travelers before a famous building. For nothing in tactile perception corresponds to what contemplation is in optical perception. ("L'Oeuvre d'art," 735–36)

As in the article on surrealism, here too contemplation gives way to a *contact* with images, and even between them. Nevertheless, the tactile immediation of the transmission and propagation of images clearly seems to be produced henceforth, not by the revolutionary utopia of the complete actuality of images, but by the market of their iconomic values. Insofar as it has incorporated the iconomic commodification of visual exchange in the form of exhibition value, insofar as it is innervated by it, the gaze constantly turns away, is dis-tracted from its object: Far from immersing itself in contemplation, it already awaits other visions. It prepares in advance to see again and again, to change sights; it is carried away in a *surplus-view* that never allows it to posit itself or become settled. And so this sight that is determined by or in exchange, this sight *of* exchange (in the double sense of an at once objective and subjective genitive), in short, this gaze that is made up of exchanges or that has become exchange is a gaze that has formed a "habit" ("L'Oeuvre d'art," 736). Which is to say that it is subject to habituation or addiction (*Gewöhnung*, Benjamin writes in the German versions):

> Tactile reception comes about not so much by way of attention as by habit.
> . . . The distracted person can form habits too. Even more, it is only when we
> master certain tasks in a state of distraction that we are certain to complete
> them by habit. (736)

Thus, like the anoptic innervation of the hand of the gambler who is accustomed to the game, perception metamorphizes, in or through film, *aisthēsis* is reorganized, and the gaze changes. As Benjamin emphasizes a few lines later: "*Reception in distraction, which . . . is a symptom of profound changes in perception, finds in film its true field of experience*" (736). Yet the new gaze, the exchange-gaze that comes to light thus, immediately and at the same time lapses into the addictive dependency of dis-traction. It is a gaze on credit, an indebted gaze.

The exchange form of the gaze that has incorporated exhibition value also makes possible the visual market in which the fiction of exchange constructs debt.

But where, then, has it gone, the innervation whose construction, whose road networks [*voirie*] we have been following to this point?

It is precisely at the moment when the word *innervation* disappears from the texture of Benjamin's text[36] that it unfolds what for us are its most crucial meanings, that is, what we might call a *political iconomy of medium*.

In the article on surrealism, on the verge of an anachronistic encounter with Deleuze, the tactility of the integral actuality of images that touch and spread took us to the very limits of the concept of the image: where there would *no longer* be any images because there would *only* be images (*no longer* [*plus*] any images because there are *always more* [*plus*] images, in a sense). And this immediation through contact that was supposed to reign within the *Bildraum* is now engendered by the traction of the distraction of exchange in what presents itself as a super- or hypermarket of the visible: If contemplation is dethroned in favor of a circulation of images that obey an always increasing speed of propagation, it is because the perfect conduction of images, as the asymptotic limit of visibility, is nothing other than the horizon of the *general and instantaneous iconomic exchange.*

This leads to an assertion that, to be sure, has an ironic aftertaste: If the innervated medium that is the space of images is thus constituted in its performative immediacy by means of another medium (recall the logic of the supplement that appeared in the reading of the 1920 fragment), if another medium is necessary to produce the immediation of the medium, then its name is henceforth what Benjamin elsewhere proposes calling, with a phrase that is no doubt a hapax legomenon in his work, the "medium of the market [*Medium des Marktes*]." Which is also to say the "money-medium [*Geldmedium*]," as Marx put it in *Capital*.[37]

There is nothing surprising, however, about the market or money thus appearing as the ultimate innervation of the space of images, for, as we have read, the iconic conduction that spreads by being discharged in that image-space obeys a logic of the unconscious: One could even say, borrowing a notion that for Freud was closely linked to that of innervation, that this space of images is a medium of immediate and integral *conversion*. Not only is this conversion in Freud a term with economic or monetary origins; in the end Benjamin himself, in a posthumous fragment from 1921 titled "Capitalism as Religion," emphasized that "Freudian theory" was "thought in entirely capitalist terms."[38]

There is no reason to be surprised, then, that where its final fires shine in the essay "The Work of Art in the Age of Its Technological Reproducibility," the motif of innervation—which has led us here by clearing a singular path through Benjamin's work—ends up allowing for a glimpse, through the transparency of the immediation of the *Bildraum*, into a monetary texture, a market innervation that ensures the incessant *convertibility* of images into actions. From the very first version of the essay on, Benjamin spoke of a "medium of perception."[39] Well, what constructs or weaves this medium is the supplementary but disappearing medium, this *surplus-medium* that is none other than the "medium of the market" or the "money-medium."

Once again, Benjamin encounters anachronistically and fleetingly—the encounter is lightning quick—Deleuze's formulation from *Time-Image*, in which "money is the reverse of all the images that the cinema shows and edits on the front."

In the paragraph that immediately follows this iconomic phrase that we have unpacked patiently, Deleuze returns to an expression that already imposed itself at the beginning of *Image-Movement*. It is also borrowed from Marx, who described money as a "general equivalent [*allgemeines Äquivalent*]." But it is the camera, in Deleuze, that is described iconomically as "a generalized equivalent of the movements of translation" (4–5). Or again as their "exchanger [*échangeur*]," a term that I understand here as relating both to money and to traffic.[40]

The camera is thus both the currency and the road switch [*aiguillage*] of movements.

What does this mean?

After a brief description of the beginning of Murnau's film *The Last Laugh* (1924), Deleuze suggests that the camera is the general equivalent of "all the means of locomotion that it shows or that it makes use of—airplane, car, boat, bicycle, foot, metro" (22). In this initial sequence, whose camera movements were entirely novel at the time, the camera in effect constructs its route by combining several means of transport one after the other; it thus engages the gaze in a succession of trajectories that are articulated with one another:

> The camera on a bicycle is put first of all in the lift, descends with it and takes in the entrance hall of a grand hotel through the glass of the window, performing constant decompositions and recompositions, then "goes through the

vestibule and through the enormous revolving door in a single and perfect tracking shot." Here the camera involves two movements, two moving bodies or two vehicles, the lift and the bicycle. (*Time-Image*, 103)[41]

We will soon look closely at elevators that, if they are open or made of glass, if one can see through them, then, decompose and recompose movement floor by floor, as Deleuze very accurately suggests: From the elevator, we have the impression of seeing a film pass by, such that an elevator, whether or not there is a camera mounted in it, is in the end already cinema. It is a cinematization of the visible, as though each floor were a still shot within a continuous scrolling movement.

What Deleuze says nothing about, however, is the revolving door, which he mentions only in passing. We will also have occasion to speak again about these doors, which I will inscribe, along with elevators and escalators, in a genealogy of the road networks of the gaze [*voiries du regard*], of which the camera is in a sense *the general surveyor* [*agent voyer general*]. But before undertaking this archaeology of the traffic networks and intersections that striate visibility, allow me to gesture, briefly, toward a remarkable appearance of the revolving door in Benjamin's article on surrealism.

Speaking of how photographic images of Parisian locales punctuate *Nadja*, the autobiographical narrative André Breton had just published the previous year, Benjamin writes: "All the parts of Paris that appear here [in the photographic reproductions that punctuate the text of *Nadja*] are places where what is between these people [between the characters of the narrative] turns like a revolving door."[42] Imagine what would happen if this revolving door [*Drehtür*] were made to turn quickly: In the eyes of those leafing through the book at great speed, *Nadja* would almost look like the folioscopes that prefigure the birth of cinema.

But the figure of the revolving door, which thus names the rotation of the images that form so many interstitial spaces between the pages of the narrative, immediately and literally becomes as big as the world. Indeed, Benjamin continues, as though there were no gap:

> All the parts of Paris that appear here are places where what is between these people turns like a revolving door.
> The Surrealists' Paris, too, is a "little universe." That is to say, in the large one, the cosmos, things look no different [*in der grossen, im Kosmos, sieht es nicht anders aus*]. There, too, there are *carrefours* [crossroads: in French in the original] where inconceivable analogies and connections between events [*unerdenkliche Analogien und Verschränkungen von Geschehnissen*] are the order of the day. (211; translation modified lightly)

The revolving door, then, is the equivalent, in the small world of the book of images, of a universal crossroad. Or again of what, with Deleuze, we might call a *general iconomic exchanger* [*échangeur*].

Did Deleuze and Benjamin cross paths somewhere in the lobby of the Atlantic Hotel in which Murnau filmed *The Last Laugh*? Might they have entered the same revolving door, perhaps without seeing each another, caught as they were in the flow of two different channels?

The fact remains that the elevator and the revolving door, which mobilize the gaze and photogrammatize the visible, produce a general cinematization of them. But they do so with a heaviness, a mechanical gravity, that Benjamin's striking innervation lacks. To be sure, we are still not in the space of images that the final pages of the essay on surrealism dreamed of, even if we are getting closer. Will the gears and cables disappear one day? Will the motivity of the gaze, will the saccades of the eyes, become immediately effective, which is to say, convertible into cash?

▷ *Deleted Scenes*: The Fluctuations of the Unchained Camera (L'Herbier).

Let's sketch out the broad outlines of a material history of the *conduits* of the visible.

A long, surprising genealogy leads from the "flying chairs" of the seventeenth century to the mechanical elevators, escalators, and sidewalks that crisscross, that chart, our movements through today's shopping malls. And these mobilizations of the gaze—we just caught a glimpse of them with

Murnau and Deleuze—cross into the world of cinema, not only in that they are staged and narrated in it, but in that they are integrated into the very routes taken by the camera, literally merging with the saccades of the cine-eye.[43] Elevatoriality, escalatoriality, as it were, thus oscillate constantly between the diegetic space of the filmic narrative that makes them visible and the metadiegetic level of the rhetoric of the movements of the camera that allows them to be represented.

I can select only a few moments, a few remarkable milestones, from the vast construction site of this ocular cinemobility. They would have to be reinscribed in a careful narrative that would take us on a journey, for example, from one of the first appearances of an escalator on screen in Chaplin's *The Floorwalker* (1916) to the memorable tracking shot on the moving sidewalk at the beginning of Tarantino's *Jackie Brown* (1997), passing by way of the mechanical stairways hauling the zombies in the shopping mall in Romero's *Dawn of the Dead* (1978). And I note only in passing that the very chronology of such a narrative, as a voyage in time, is not external to the history narrated, does not look down on it from a historical reason that is external to it, for the temporal shift also depends on these mobilizations of the gaze in its possibility as in its chronometric measure.[44]

Searching for the elevator's forerunner, then, one can go back at least to the "flying chairs" whose invention is often attributed to the French nobleman and member of the Académie Française, Jean-Jacques Renouard de Villayer, but which seem to have been installed in various palaces even earlier, notably that of Cardinal Mazarin.[45] Upon the request of Louis XV, a personal elevator of this kind, with pulleys, ropes, and counterweights, was built in Versailles in 1743 by Blaise-Henri Arnoult, who also designed the stage equipment for the Royal Opera of Versailles. The elevator was intended for Madame de Châteauroux, a favorite of the king, who used it to get to her rooms on the third floor.

In 1691, in an augmented edition of his *Characters*, which first appeared in 1688, La Bruyère paints the portrait of Hermippus, for which Villayer, some say, might have been the model.[46] Hermippus, La Bruyère writes, "is the slave of what he calls little conveniences [*commodités*]," but he is "a great master of springs and mechanics," who "draws light for his apartment from places other than the window," and who "found the secret of going up and down by means other than the stairs." This space could be described as Hermippean: It is equipped with artificial lights and a novel form of circulation intended to make it more convenient.

Nevertheless, we have to wait for the middle of the nineteenth century for elevators to become vectors not only of the mobilization of the gaze but of the commodification of public space. In 1854, its inventor, Elisha Otis, gave a demonstration of the reliability of a mechanized elevator equipped with a parachute brake system. The event took place in New York's Crystal Palace, home to the World's Fair, which had opened the previous year. In a dramatic gesture,[47] Otis cut the cable that appeared to be holding the platform on which he himself was standing. His gesture caused a big stir, and clients flocked, among them the big department stores: that of Eder V. Haughwout, at the corner of Broadway and Broome Street, which specialized in porcelain and glassware, was in 1857 the first to be equipped with an Otis elevator.

From that point on, the elevator and the department store seem to develop a sort of symbiosis, with the elevator forming a closed but mobile conduit within the department store, a moving interiority inside the vast commercial interior. Thus, in 1883, in *The Ladies' Delight*,[48] Zola describes two elevators "padded with velvet" that Mouret, the owner of the department store that gives the novel its name, has installed:

> Madame Bourdelais was looking around for a staircase when she saw one of the lifts and pushed the children into it. . . . Madame Marty and Valentine also got into the narrow lift where everyone was tightly packed, but the mirrors, the velvet-covered seats and the moulded bronze doors kept them so occupied that they reached the first floor without feeling the machine slide gently upwards.

Even when it is the site of a collective journey, the elevator, if it is not open and made of wire netting like the one in *The Last Laugh*, is a passage hidden from view; it keeps something of the "secret" of Hermippus's "flying chair." Its trajectory is *volée* in both senses of the word: On the one hand, it is fast and aerial; on the other hand, it is hidden; it tends to go unseen. Perhaps there is even, inherent in the trajectory of the elevator, the promise of a secret floor that only I can reach.

We see this ghost floor toward which every elevator might well secretly be under way in a wonderful episode of the series *The Twilight Zone* titled "The After Hours" that appeared on June 10, 1960. The protagonist, a young woman by the name of Marsha White, stands in line with other clients in front of one of the two elevators in a department store, to take it to the housewares department, where she hopes to find the gold thimble she's looking for. But the second elevator arrives: Marsha sees the elevator operator signal to her to get right in, and she is surprised by the special treatment, as though all of a sudden she had her own elevator, a sort of flying chair for her own private use. She had set out, as the voice-over puts it, on "a most prosaic, ordinary, run-of-the-mill errand," but soon finds herself in the specialties department, on the ninth floor of a department store that . . . only has eight.

Up there, there is nothing but the one and only article Marsha was looking for. As though the department, as though the floor, were entirely for her, *specially* for her. Marsha tells the saleswoman who seems always to have been waiting to provide her with the very object of her quest, "That's odd, you haven't any merchandise here at all, except the thimble, except the very thing I needed." The elevator in this episode of *The Twilight Zone* thus carries its passenger to the consumerist phantasmagoria par excellence: that mass consumer goods can be intended not for everyone but specifically for each of us in our singularity, in our unicity.

La Bruyère, as you recall, describing Hermippus and how he "climbed and descended other than by using the stairs," said he was "the slave of . . . little conveniences," among which he clearly counted the flying chair, the forerunner of the elevator. "Conveniences [*commodités*]" here means things that are "pleasant, agreeable": This is the meaning the *Littré* gives, citing precisely the first sentence of the portrait of Hermippus. But "commodités," as Antoine Furetière's *Dictionnaire universel* points out in 1690, are also, in a now archaic sense of the French word, *commodities* (English having kept this meaning for products or merchandise). And so for Marsha it is as though her elevator—the elevator made for her, suited to her, *commodus* in Latin—came and went, as though it went up and down, between these very two meanings, between the comfort of ease and the consumer good suited to her unique desire.

But what happens to this *com-modifying* elevator when it has an openwork door, when you can see through its metallic grill? Murnau's open elevator appears again later in the opening credits of *The Big Store* (1941), where the vertical scrolling of the images—the very movement of cinematographic projection, in which frames follow one another on the film as it unspools—is superimposed upon, and merges very precisely with, the trajectory of the elevator car: As the spectator watches the credits, his point of view climbs from one image to the next, as though it were rising from floor to floor in the stock of commodities for sale, and the cinematography of the gaze matches the ascending mechanism, that of the shopper climbing the levels of the consumer sanctuary. All the way to this final ghost floor that, if it existed, would stop all movement, for the gaze would immediately coincide with its one and only phantasmatic object.

Of course, many opening credits make this articulation, this connection that—since this is the role of credits—undertake to synchronize, *to mesh*, the gaze of the spectator with the scrolling of the film. It should suffice here to recall the opening of *Rear Window* (1954), where the initial static shot of the upward movement of the three window blinds in Jeff's (James Stewart) apartment gives way to the camera tracking forward; once it has arrived at the window sill, the camera goes down into the courtyard below, following a cat climbing the stairs before leaving it to climb the rungs of a fire escape. But what is remarkable in *The Big Store* is that the mobilization of the gaze is explicitly placed under the sign of the elevator and the shop at the same time. As though the gaze itself ended up among the *commodités*, in the two possible senses of this word: On the one hand, like Hermippus's flying chair, the film spectator's gaze is also mechanized, integrated into the motor system that is supposed to facilitate its movement; and, on the other hand, it becomes reified

▷ *Deleted Scenes*: The General Fetishism of the Marxes.

▷ *Deleted Scenes*: The Amortization of the Gaze (*King Kong*).

merchandise, a good or valuable, one *commodity* among others in the exchange of goods. In this way, it begins to be inscribed in the iconomic super-market.

This *commodification* of the gaze is what we must now try to grasp by turning to mechanisms related to the elevator and which, like it, and even better than it, mobilize our view while also subjecting it to an iconomy of vision.

In 1859, Nathan Ames filed the patent for revolving stairs, mechanical stairs moving in a permanent revolution, as it were.[49] He himself described them as "an endless inclined flight of steps," which "shall serve as elevators." And he sees them being used to "render the upper stories of large buildings comparatively easy of access," so that "their value will be greatly enhanced." It is thus a matter of valorizing space and the flow within that space.

The invention of revolving stairs did not lead to the production of any known model of escalator. Not until the patent filed by Jesse W. Reno in 1892 did the escalator as we know it begin to make its appearance in the urban landscape.[50] Reno insists that his "endless conveyor or elevator," which is capable of transporting "six thousand passengers per hour," can be installed in large numbers and so as to ensure continuous flow:

> One or one set of conveyers . . . may be run to elevate from one floor-level to another, and one or one set of elevators, with their hand-rails, may be run to descend and convey passengers from one floor-level to a lower level, so that there will be no stopping of the conveyers and no change of direction in their movements, and crowds or streams of persons may pass each other in opposite directions without confusion or detention.

The important thing, the principal contribution of the mechanism, is thus the uninterrupted continuity of flow, in Ames as in Reno. As an employee of Marshall Field's department store in Chicago will later say, "Escalators bring circulation to the upper stories, like blood to the veins."[51]

Reno and Ames, as we have just seen, used the word *elevator* to describe their respective inventions. Some years later, at the 1900 World's Fair in Paris, another inventor, Charles Seeberger, in association with the elevator manufacturer Otis, introduced the first commercial *escalator*, a name he had just registered as a trademark.[52] In the meantime, in London, clients at Harrods could already circulate on mechanical stairs, installed in 1898 (when they got to the top, the story goes, a house-steward was waiting with a brandy to help them recover from the fright). And soon there was a frantic race among the department stores to see which would be outfitted with the most escalators. This escalation of general escalatorization produces dizzying figures for the time: In 1927, Gimbels in New York boasted that its twenty-seven escalators could transport the equivalent of a city in an hour; the following year, Bamberger's in Newark proudly boasted of its thirty-four escalators circulating throughout twenty floors.[53]

From the department store in which it proliferates, we quite soon find the escalator back in cinema. As I mentioned, it made one of its first appearances on screen in 1916 in Chaplin's *The Floorwalker*. There, we see Charlie, who, trying to escape the men following him, takes a mechanical staircase the wrong way and runs in place, until he finally takes the elevator to change floors and exit the film, which thus comes to an end.

Running while standing still: This paradoxical movement around which Chaplin's gag revolves is that of the permanent revolution ("endless revolving") of the escalator, the uninterrupted fluidity its inventors, Ames and Reno, already emphasized. In a later film such as *A Matter of Life and Death*, directed by Michael Powell and Emeric Pressburger in 1946, this infinite loop is in a sense used as the endless trajectory the giant mechanical staircase traces between our world and the beyond (the film appeared with the title *Stairway to Heaven* in the United States).

Circulating in the history of cinema, we could stop our time machine (maybe a chronological elevator?) at more recent scenes. I have in mind one of the most remarkable moments in the filmography of the escalator, the closing scene of *Carlito's Way* (Brian De Palma, 1993). There, we see the protagonist, Carlito Brigante (Al Pacino), who is trying to flee the Italian Mafiosi chasing him. And a mechanical staircase in New York's Grand Central Station becomes the theater for a memorable series of revolutions or circumvolutions in a long sequence of virtuoso shots filmed with a Steadicam.[54] Twice Carlito is about to take the escalator but stops and abruptly turns around at the last moment when he sees one of the men following him at the bottom.

The first time, the camera following him also backs up and goes with him as he hides around a corner. The second time, however, the camera lets him turn back by himself, lets him leave the frame, itself taking the down escalator, as though its movement, freed from Carlito's and become autonomous, had merged with that of the mobile staircase.[55] It thus ends up on the lower level, with the Mafiosi. There, it rotates slowly, climbing back up with one of them in the other direction, thus heading again toward the upper floor where Carlito is to be found. Barely interrupted by two insert shots, the camera's climb takes us closer and closer to the gaze of the Mafioso. We are about to get a close-up of his eyes when, suddenly, the shot swerves to the right and shows the down escalator beside it. On it, we see Carlito, lying on the steps, almost invisible, in the process of leaving the scene unnoticed. De Palma then brings this long take to an end and alternates rapidly between highly contrasted shots. The camera takes the point of view of the prostrate Carlito, briefly watching the Mafioso who is going up without seeing him; then it stops mid-floor to take a medium long shot of the passengers on the two escalators and, finally, rises for a high angle shot of Carlito's descent, viewed from on high, from ever higher up, as though our point of view were getting further away by being carried away on an elevator.

What happens in this masterfully composed sequence just before the gunfight breaks out? Carlito seems to hesitate to enter into the loop of the infinite revolution of the escalators. But the camera frees itself from its character and willingly allows itself to be taken, to mesh with the uninter-rupted flow of the escalatorial machine. Its movement, which attracts our gaze, is geared into these conveyors, into these drive belts that carry passengers.

Nevertheless, one has the impression that it is a question, for the character Carlito as for the camera that films him, precisely of getting out of the inexo-rable loop of visual circulation. It is as though Carlito were trying to get off at the bottom, while the camera climbs ever higher, trying to escape at the top. Its ascension, which is symmetrical to the posture of the protagonist clinging to the steps as though trying to push his way into them, seeks to form a powerful vertical axis opposite to the closed circuit of the escalators.

Is something like the "dialectic" Fredric Jameson analyzed in the atrium of the famous Bonaventure Hotel in Los Angeles at work in this fascinating sequence? Jameson describes the flight of the elevator as the promise of a potential escape that ends up being denied:[56]

> Yet the escalator and elevator are also in this context dialectical opposites; and we may suggest that the glorious movement of the elevator gondolas is also a dialectical compensation for this filled space of the atrium—it gives us the chance at a radically different, but complementary, spatial experience, that of rapidly shooting up through the ceiling and outside. . . . But even this vertical movement is contained: the elevator lifts you to one of those revolving cocktail lounges, in which you, seated, are again passively rotated about and offered a contemplative spectacle of the city itself, now transformed into its own images by the glass windows through which you view it.[57]

Does this same dialectic guide De Palma's camera? And can we speak of a dialectic here, even a negative or thwarted one?

Everything turns, everything circulates, in department stores and com-mercial centers, in atriums or shopping malls, which are constructed as spaces of permanent revolution: One enters them through the *revolving doors* we have already come across in Murnau (the turnstile-like doors were patented in the United States in 1888),[58] one circulates through them from floor to floor on *revolving stairs* (the escalators I am emphasizing to such a degree), one enters into infinitely renewable debts called *revolving credit*. . . .

In this sense, Rem Koolhaas and his students in the Harvard Project on the City are right to analyze the escalator as a vector of the general smoothness of space ("escalator = smoothness," they write) that allows for the limitless development of shopping:

> As opposed to the elevator, which is limited in terms of the numbers it can transport between different floors and which through its very mechanism insists on division, the escalator accommodates and combines any flow, efficiently creates smooth transitions between one level and another, and even blurs the distinction between separate levels and individual spaces. The escalator radically modifies architecture; it denies the relevance of both compartments and floors. The success and rapid acceptance of the escalator—which effectively enabled the department store at the beginning of the twentieth century—is due to its effortless ability to transform virtual space into retail area.[59]

Of course, extending well beyond department stores, inundating shopping malls with its continual flow, the escalator proliferates endlessly in cities, invading urban space: "There are three hundred thousand of them in the world, and they double in number every ten years," Koolhaas declared in an interview in 2001. It would be a mistake, however, to place the escalator and the elevator in opposition as he does and to isolate the escalator within what would appear, rather, to be a *general mobilization*, which we will get a better idea of with this other statistic: *Altogether*, all the elevators, escalators, and other moving sidewalks in the world would move the equivalent of the population of the earth every three days.[60]

From our iconomic perspective, it is the connections and assemblages of escalators, moving sidewalks, and elevators—especially since the appearance of external and glass, that is, panoramic elevators[61]—that form a general road network [*voirie*] of the visible and thus allow the gazes they transport to mesh with the slide rails that are the equivalent, for so-called natural perception, of the cranes and other dollies that arrange the cinegaze. Above, below, across: The mechanization of movement on rails that striate space in all directions goes hand in hand with so many road switches [*aiguillages*] of the gaze that Brian De Palma—him again!—orchestrates in a remarkable scene from *Body Double* (1984).

What do we see in this Los Angeles shopping mall where Jake Scully (Craig Wasson) follows the mysterious Gloria Revelle (Deborah Shelton), the woman he was watching the previous evening with a telescope from his apartment? Jake follows Gloria and gets on the escalator behind her. The camera follows them, thus also getting in sync with the movement of the mechanical staircase, merging with it as it will do nine years later in *Carlito's Way*. Once at the next floor, Gloria and Jake head for a second escalator. But this time, the camera films them from above in a long zoom out that moves from a medium to a wide-angle shot: Little by little, we see the whole mall, in which we also see a panoramic elevator going up. And the camera's optical movement back and upward takes place on a remarkable axis: Our gaze seems, on the one hand, to be borne by vertical tracks, as though it had climbed into an elevator that is the double of the one we just saw go up; and, on the other hand, it goes backward while remaining directed at Jake and Gloria down below, so that the zooming out traces an oblique line, a diagonal that appears symmetrical to that of the escalator we are observing.

Why emphasize, as I do here, these details, this virtuoso but apparently insignificant play of camera movements De Palma dreams up? Because the director's camera itself becomes a sort of *body double*: a stand-in [*doublure*] for *both* the elevator and the escalator. An undecidable stand-in [*doublure*], then, doubling either one but also the one as the other, without offering an external point of view that would allow us to imagine an *outside* to the transportation system of the gaze. Ourselves caught up in them, we see these optical displacements and exchanges; we observe the escalator or elevator from an elevator or escalator, even from a *general lift* [*élévateur*] that partakes of both without ever succeeding in exceeding them, without ever managing to *sublate* them in a third, overarching term.

In short, there is undoubtedly no dialectic in the common sense in this economy of gazes of which the mall De Palma films becomes the theater. There are eyes that slide over slide rails, that seem to move away, to distance themselves so as to double and redouble one another, to exchange places within a general and permanent revolution none of the gazes escape.

We cannot simply leave the cinema or the shopping mall by putting them in opposition to a nonmechanized gaze or virgin spaces that would not fall within what Rem Koolhaas calls *junkspace*.[62] In other words, there is no—or no longer any—view *outside the market* (if there ever was one). And all the less so since the commercial network of vision continues outside-film and outside-the-mall.

Indeed, we are today witness to a novel development of all kinds of eye-tracking technologies and video-elevation mechanisms. Well beyond the cinema and shopping malls, there are "elevators" everywhere on the screens that are part of our daily gestures. And the commercial applications of eye tracking—an abyssal expression, if we listen to it, since we can hear in it at once the eye that is tracked or followed and the eye equipped with rails or tracks—these applications are spreading, on the internet and elsewhere.[63]

On May 27, 2013, an advertisement in the Swiss version of the free daily paper *20 Minutes* (20min.ch) echoed the following marketing event:

> On Thursday, May 16, 2013, in the central Zurich train station, the passersby had the chance to win a Samsung Galaxy S4 simply by using their eyes. Anyone who could look at the new smartphone for an hour without diverting their eyes would walk away with the phone! But it wasn't as easy as all that: a single blink of the eye to the side, however brief, and all was lost!

The smartphone in question in fact detects the user's eye movements, allowing the user to control the *smart scroll* function with just the eyes (to scroll through a text on the screen, for example). In other words, the gaze itself here becomes, immediately, an elevator or lift, even (why not?) an escalator or travelator.

This advertising campaign is a sign or symptom of the advanced stage, of the degree of development, the commercial innervation of the gaze that

Benjamin spoke of has reached today. We can also get a sense of this from Harun Farocki's remarkable film *Die Schöpfer der Einkaufswelten* (*The Creators of Shopping Worlds*, 2001), in which the director interviews engineers, architects, and marketers working on the plans for a shopping mall. The scene of the calibrating of the eye of a potential client in order to calculate the points of ocular impact within the plethora of signs, posters, and commercial stimulations of all kinds that cover the gallery walls in this consumerist den recalls the moment in *Jackie Brown* where the title character stops for a moment at the entrance of the Del Amo Mall, in the small city of Torrance, close to Los Angeles: We then see the system of mechanical mobilizations of the gaze formed by the elevator and escalator channeling the flow of shoppers; then, in a reverse angle shot that shows us the protagonist's eyes, we observe their saccades, which seem to repeat the same mechanized movements.[64]

In addition to these instant routings of the gaze, the advertising campaign for the smartphone reacting to our slightest glances also suggested something else. With the challenge it presented, that of an apparently innocent game or competition, it signified not only that the space in which our gaze moves is marked out, all its trajectories charted. It also declared that this gaze, because it works, because it represents *working time*, that is, one hour of captive attention, produces value.[65]

In other words, the commercial stakes of the current image media, of which this smartphone is but one example, are not only that the gaze itself becomes the general equivalent of the means of locomotion, as Deleuze said in speaking of the camera, of this cinematographic mechanism that innervates our eyes; they are also, and above all, what he described as dissymmetrical exchange, exchange without equivalence: "giving the image for money," to be sure, but also, into the bargain, "giving time for images" (*Time-Image*, 78).

General innervation through elevation, this ocular grafting that in the end forms the very texture of a gaze on the rails of exchangism within the super(-)market of the visible is thus the mechanism that makes possible the valorization of iconomic capital: The gaze at work creates surplus-value— *surplus-view*, we might say—to the precise extent to which it constitutes supplemental work, without either exchange or equivalent.

▷ *Formats*: Surplus-Definition (*Redacted*).

Additional Features

Merchandise

Godzilla's Eye

"Size Does Matter": This catchphrase served as the pitch for the *Godzilla* directed by Roland Emmerich in 1998. The slogan, according to Dean Devlin, co-writer and producer of the film, seems to have been landed on during a meeting with the marketing directors from Sony Pictures Entertainment, who "asked a very legitimate question":

> They said: "If I've already seen *Jurassic Park*, why do I need to see *Godzilla*? Haven't I already seen the big lizard movie?" And that's when a very clever marketing executive said, "Well, size does matter."[1]

The size of what?

The size of the monster, of course, the size of what the film promises to show with its filmic monstration. That is, the size of Godzilla himself, who becomes something like the metonymy of the blockbuster that he inhabits, that he carries, and that carries him: Giving his name at once to the protagonist and to the film that contains him, Godzilla must become the tautegorical sign of his own size, which aims to surpass that of his predecessors, especially the dinosaurs in *Jurassic Park*. A size measured also by his relative height compared to the most famous landmarks of the urban space: An article that appeared in *Fortune* shortly after the film was released in May of 1998 reported on how the Sony publicists placed billboards close to monuments in American cities, announcing, for example, next to the bridge itself, that "he's [the monster] as tall as the Brooklyn Bridge."[2]

In counterpoint to this conquest of size, every self-respecting blockbuster also has to miniaturize itself by offering a range of tie-in products derived from the film on countless media. Thus, the same *Fortune* article describes the commercial war that raged in order to create distribution paths for the film:

> The blitz of information [yes, blitz: this is the language of war, of the military, of *Blitzkrieg*] about *Godzilla* isn't confined to the media, of course; it's also made its way to your corner market, where 3,000 products bearing Godzilla logos, including Hershey bars, Duracell batteries, and an ice-cream flavor called Godzilla Vanilla, now await you. . . . To that end Taco Bell . . . has committed some $60 million to promoting the movie—and, of course, its own wares. . . . When a movie works, it creates an aura . . . around itself that extends to everything it touches.
>
> This is especially true in the area of product placement, where specific brands are strategically inserted into the film itself. For *Godzilla*, Workman [Mark Workman, Sony's senior vice president for strategic marketing] has lined up placements for Swatch watches and Kodak cameras.

But we also see other brands in *Godzilla*, especially the American video rental chain, Blockbuster Video, whose yellow and blue logo appears several times during an eventful sequence that takes place in the aisles of Madison Square Garden. The scientist Niko Tatopoulos (Matthew Broderick) is being chased, along with a few others, by little monsters, Godzilla's babies, which are barely hatched, have just left the egg. And so, in front of the word BLOCKBUSTER, written in capital letters, literally against the background of this signifier, Nick, who has stayed back a bit, defies the Babyzillas by knocking down a rack of balls and a bubble gum machine. The proliferating little monsters trip, fall over one another, get mixed in with the countless scattered consumer products, forming what looks like a real cascade of merchandise. Before our eyes, and before the eyes of Nick, who in the meantime has taken cover behind a protective wall, the blockbuster seems to break into pieces and become monetized, to divide itself infinitely in order to reproduce itself.

Exchange and monetization do not simply await the blockbuster once it *comes out*, as the saying goes, on the mass market of broadcasting and distribution. Even before it *comes out*, in itself then, the blockbuster is already the theater of multiple circulations of exchange. Or perhaps one should say (and this no doubt amounts to the same thing) that it will have internalized its outside in advance, that is, the scene of its monetization. It does not simply wait for it, then, over there, on the outside.

Godzilla, we know, did not turn out to be the success it was expected to be. With the $375 million it brought in at the box office, the film did not live up to expectations in terms of return on investment, leaving it third among the 1998 blockbusters, after *Armageddon* and *Saving Private Ryan*. A (relative) failure that the director Roland Emmerich attributed to the exaggerated marketing, the outlandish media and commercial hype orchestrated by Sony.[3]

This is perhaps why, despite its poor box office results, *Godzilla* has become a sort of emblem of the commercial film par excellence. Thus, in *What Just Happened*, a comedy directed by Barry Levinson in 2008, clearly with the intent to denounce current Hollywood practices, what seems to count as the metonymy for blockbusters in general is *Godzilla*'s eye—or at least the eye of a big generic (in the same way we speak of generic drugs) lizard.

Ben (Robert De Niro), an ageing Hollywood producer, and Jeremy Brunell (Michael Wincott), an intransigent director who holds himself in high esteem, sit in the waiting room of the office of a female producer who is about to meet them in order to negotiate—or rather, to impose—a new ending for the movie they have just filmed and edited. On the wall: a poster out of which the eye of the giant reptile looks at them.

An eye and a number: $810 million. Ben comments: "In the end, no director, no stars, not even a title. Just a number. A big number."

Ben's disillusioned commentary is inscribed in a triangular exchange of gazes between him, the director, and the Eye of capital. And so the poster doesn't just hang over the people seated under it, as though they were under its imperative, imposed from on high or beyond: It is not, as the film, with its naïve critique of Hollywood, would have us believe, a simple external law, a constraint of the economic reality to which one has to accommodate oneself as best one can. And from which one could easily free oneself by opting, perhaps, for an economy parallel to mass cinema and its exigencies of production.

It would indeed be worthwhile analyzing all the trajectories, charting all the directions, the actors' eyes take here. Ben fixes his gaze on the eye of the poster, then turns toward Jeremy, who is also looking at the poster. Close-up of Ben, who lowers his eyes, lifts them, sighs, lowers them again. Close-up of Jeremy, whose gaze, clearly, is directed or aimed, alternately, at Ben and the poster, oscillating from one to the other. Close-up, again, of the Eye of the cyclops above the number, *from which* the camera proceeds, this time, to a reverse-angle shot toward the producer and director sitting on the sofa looking at each other, exchanging looks of understanding as Ben offers his skeptical commentary. And finally, close-up, once again, of Jeremy fixing his gaze on the cycloptic eye that is fixed on him.

If money—the amount displayed in dollars—is here the sign that the film is a market of values, it also seems to designate *that which animates gazes*. That which puts them into circulation as points of view that, they too, are exchanged and have value one for the other, one for the other.

Just as *Godzilla* (the film) is exchanged for chocolate bars, batteries, or watches; just as Godzilla (the protagonist in the film) is exchanged for countless Babyzillas who themselves likewise seem to be exchanged for hundreds of balls or millions of gumballs; well, so too (*just as*, *so too* being the very formula for analogy that, itself, is also exchange, proportion, calculation . . .), yes, so too the very gazes are inscribed in a network of exchange within which they take on and give value.

Deleted Scenes

Doors and Slide Changers in *Pickpocket* and *Obsession*

Money, in Bresson's *Money*, goes through the door, the threshold of the film, to enter into the film. And we get the sense that the door it goes through is more than a simple door: With its repeated closings, it seems to produce *coupures* (understood in both senses, as naming at once *banknotes* and filmic interruption, a *cut*, editing).

The closed door of the ATM and the glass door of Norbert's father's office, the sliding door of the machine for dispensing banknotes-images [*débiter des coupures-images*] and the gate to the prison where Yvon is locked up . . . Whether open or closed, doors are an important motif in the work of Bresson, who describes their role in rhythmic terms: "Doors," he declares, "have above all a musical meaning . . . thanks to the rhythm they impose." And he adds: "This rhythm is the rhythm that belongs to the film, in which they function like the separations between movements or musical bars."[1]

Doors thus measure movement, they punctuate the stream of images, as we can see in exemplary fashion in *Pickpocket*, where Bresson is forever linking series of doors, whether open, closed, or ajar.

Thus, when Michel is arrested at the races and then released because of a lack of evidence, the gesture of his hand grasping the bills the police detective offers him seems to trigger a whole series of doors: the door to the office and then that to the entrance of the police station (which itself provides the frame for another door, further inside); the door to the building Michel lives in; the door to his room. After fading to the blackness of Michel falling asleep and the narrative ellipsis that shows him in the following shot, in the morning, climbing down from the rear platform of a bus (though not without turning around, as though he were passing through a revolving door), the syncopated phrasing of this consecution from door to door starts over: Michel enters his mother's building (a short tracking shot follows him until the camera stops in order to show the frame of the open front door) and climbs the stairs (first we see an empty landing, then he enters the frame); he arrives at the door to his mother's apartment and, as he hesitates before knocking or ringing ("it had been more than a month since I had seen my mother; I hesitated"), another door opens, one floor down, in Jeanne's apartment. "Wait," she calls to Michel, but her voice is suspended, interrupted between the verb and its object by the opening and closing of the door, which thus appears at once as a punctuation of the spoken phrase ("Wait—the key, I was going to open the door for you") and what Dziga Vertov called the film-phrase, that is, essentially, editing.[2]

The doors follow one another, door after door, as though action and character were about to disappear, since they are nothing more than a pretext for showing a sequence of passages or thresholds, that is, transit as such, the very passing of images.

Indeed, let's imagine that Bresson's film-phrase—with its doors marking and punctuating movement like musical bars—sped up to reach the limit of a pure door-to-door. What would happen? In the end, we would no doubt reach a sort of perfect coincidence between the door as the object filmed and what one might call *inter-images*: The door would become the passage through which a filmic image moves in order to exchange places with, to be substituted for, another image.

This door that makes or allows images to go through is precisely what the opening credit sequence in Brian De Palma's *Obsession* (1976) portrays. There, we see, first, the slow tracking of the camera as it climbs the steps of the Basilica San Miniato al Monte, its climb regularly interrupted by slides taken of Michael Courtland (Cliff Robertson) and his wife Elizabeth (Geneviève Bujold) when they first met in Florence in 1948. Then, by way of an intercut, we find ourselves in New Orleans in 1959, and another forward tracking shot, this one just as slow, carries our gaze to Michael and Elizabeth's luxurious home, where they are celebrating their tenth wedding anniversary with their friends. This time, the images of the slide show of their souvenir photographs seem to glide over the glass door of the house; we see nothing of the outside, only the intermittent rhythm, the alternation between light and dark in the movement from one projection to another.

The door is thus presented in *Obsession* as what is called a slide changer [*passe-vues*]: a pre-cinematographic mechanism like the magic lantern that appeared in the seventeenth century and that makes images go by, ensures their perpendicular gliding across the projection plane, so that they exchange places, one following the other.

But there aren't only doors. Cinema has a thousand ways of representing, remarking, or reinscribing on screen this passage of sights, this transaction or transit of frames that its writing of movement consists in. For example, still in *Obsession*, there is a beautiful sequence in which Michael, after his wife and daughter have been kidnapped, boards a boat with a briefcase full of bills intended for their kidnappers (counterfeit bills, the voiceover explains as the boat pulls out). The camera then remains at length on the paddle wheel, which first looks like a sort of slide carousel, then, when seen in close-up, like a mechanism for stirring the flow of images.

Obsession could be described, essentially, as a masterful staging of different speeds in the exchange between images. The fastest is that mixer of images that is the paddle wheel, while the slowest is no doubt the altarpiece that Sandra (the daughterly double of Elizabeth) is in the process of restoring in the Basilica di San Miniato al Monte: Flaking off from all the humidity, the paint allows another painting to appear beneath it, a sort of phantom-image that had been covered over by the other paint.

Whether they change places every millisecond or have to wait several centuries, images, from the point of view of a general iconomy, have value only in view of one another. And that is why we have to say over and over that there are no images, only the relationships between them.

▷ *Photo Gallery:* Blow-Up, or Why There Are No Images.

Deleted Scenes

Three Variations on Time and Money
(Antonioni, De Palma, Bresson)

So many films have staged, each in its own way, the proverb "time is money."

In a scene in Antonioni's *Eclipse* (1962) filmed at the Rome stock exchange, a minute of silence is requested to pay homage to a colleague who died that same morning. Under the screen displaying the stock prices, the crowd of traders stands still and silent. No one moves or says a word. But this unheard of silence—highly improbable in this, the noisiest place possible—is punctuated by the long rings of telephones constantly going off. We of course imagine impatient, desperate investors calling insistently. But it's hard not to think that it's the market, the market itself, that is calling, that makes phone calls to its actors to get them moving again, to shake them from their immobility and mutism.

Antonioni's camera alternates between shots of the bodies and of the frozen faces of the traders, following a tight, quick rhythm that seems to be dictated by the telephone calls ringing in the void. It is as though the cine-matographic montage broke loose and freed itself from any narrative pre-text, as though it obeyed only a phrasing whose sole purpose—no one's purpose—is the security prices that continue to fluctuate as time passes.

Indeed, when Piero (Alain Delon) whispers, in an aside to Vittoria (Monica Vitti), that "a minute here costs billions [*un minuto qua costa mil-liardi*]," we can't tell which minute he's talking about. Of course, Piero seems to be talking about the minute of silence he is experiencing, the one the film represents and narrates as taking place at the Rome stock exchange. But since the part of the film that shows this minute also lasts a minute, it is as though the film were displacing the question of the value of time onto another plane: no longer in the diegesis but in the very experience of screening, in the experience of the spectators we are. We too participate in the fluctuation of narrative values during this minute in which every stable anchoring in a narrative is suspended: We live a pure filmic *speculation* on the passage of time.

This leap from one level to another—this metalepsis, to put it in the language of narratology—is also what takes place in a beautiful scene from *Scarface*, the film directed by Brian De Palma in 1983.[1] In it, we see Tony Montana (Al Pacino) counting the money he brings in dealing drugs. And Seidelbaum, who launders this dirty money while working secretly for the police, is also counting. Seidelbaum puts the bills in a machine, at the other side of which Tony takes them out in small piles of equal value. The piles in question are then gathered together in boxes, one of which carries the trademarked name of a business that seems to manufacture film reels (*Reel Tape Corp.*). As though the bills, reeled off one by one and grouped together, were supposed to come together to make a series of frames, as though the banknotes-images [*images-coupures*]—fiduciary money—formed the folio-scope of a film that is in the process of being made.[2]

While Tony and Seidelbaum differ over the grand total of the operation, the camera moves slowly to the clock that overlooks the scene from the wall it hangs on. As we move toward it, we see that, instead of the number 12 at the top of the dial, there is a black hole, an empty space. The camera freezes: We see what time it is—11:06 p.m.—before a dissolve impercepti-bly moves the hands to 1:32. Time has passed. The camera pulls back; we hear the characters, tired at this late hour, yawning. Then, suddenly, Sei-delbaum and his enforcer pull out their guns as two cops enter the room. Pointing to the dial, he asks Tony, who finds himself under arrest, "You see that eye there in the clock?" The camera moves closer to the clock again and, in a sort of vertiginous reverse-angle shot, shows another cop who, on the other side of the clock dial, through the midnight hole, watches and records the scene on a video monitor. What the screen (within the screen) shows, what is inscribed retrospectively on the back of each image we have just seen as if to account for it, is the *time code* of the film (of the film) that will have been made thus.

This verso on which the accounting for time and money are superim-posed on each other is also what seems to fascinate the characters in Bres-son's *Money*. In a sequence that follows soon after the initial opening and closing of the ATM and Norbert's short dialogue with his father about the debt he has run up at school, we see the young man at the house of his friend Martial, desperately trying to find a way to repay the money he has borrowed. Norbert sets his watch on the desk, with the clear intention of using it as guarantee. He would like to pawn time—or at least the meton-ymy of time that clocks are—against money. But Martial pushes the watch away and, in its place, shows Norbert a five hundred Franc bill (the "Pas-cal," with Blaise Pascal imprinted on its recto and verso). "Look," he says to him, "what do you think?" And Norbert responds, *turning the bill over*, "Nothing."

"It's a counterfeit," Martial says laconically, in that famous flat, neutral voice that is characteristic of Bresson's "models," as he preferred to call his actors. As Norbert leafs through an album Martial has just handed him—it's full of reproductions of works of art—they decide to "invest" the banknote, that is, to exchange it for real money, by going to a photo shop (a detail Bresson picks up from Tolstoy's novella *The Forged Coupon*, which the film is a loose adaptation of). Martial tells the shop owner: "We would like a small frame: nice, not too expensive." And so the two boys exchange their counterfeit bill for an empty frame—a frame in which any picture could be inserted interchangeably—thus setting in motion the spate of consequences that will lead inexorably to Yvon being put in jail, then to the final massacre punctuating his descent to hell. On the way, Norbert and the photographer will also partake in the game of *turning* the "Pascal" *over and over, recto and verso*, holding it up to the light, testing its value by looking through it.

Exchanging time—the time of debt—for counterfeit money that is exchanged in turn for a frame that can accommodate interchangeable images: This is what sets the filmic narrative of Bresson's *Money* in motion. But the characters seem always to want to see the other side of the film, where time is money, or vice versa.

Photo Gallery

Blow-Up, or Why There Are No Images

"No pictures."

If I had to pick out one line from Antonioni's masterly *Blow-Up* (1966), it would be this one, which comes during an exchange between the fashion photographer, Thomas (David Hemmings), and an elderly man who owns an antiques shop near the park where the picture of a murder will be taken:

—What do you want?
—Just looking around.
—There are no cheap bargains here, you're wasting your time.
—Well, I'll just have a look.
—What are you looking for?
—Pictures.
—No pictures. What kind of pictures?
—Landscapes.
—Sorry, no landscapes. Sold. All sold.

The antiques dealer is the first to speak, addressing Thomas, who is looking at the objects for sale. No pictures to buy, he says in a tone that is at once bored and peremptory to the man who is there *to see*. No pictures to be had for a good price, even *no pictures at all*. But what pictures, he adds, immediately contradicting himself with a question that is almost an offer.

If this singular retort insists and persists in my memory of the film, it is no doubt because it signals an iconomic motif that traverses the film both discreetly and incessantly. Thomas suggests he might buy a picture, a painting, a sort of pointillist Pollock from Bill, the young abstract painter who is staying with his partner, Patricia, next door to Thomas. A

bit later, as he makes two young models wait (one of them is Jane Birkin), Thomas plays at length with a coin between his fingers. He responds to Jane (Vanessa Redgrave), who wants to get back compromising photos Thomas took of her with a man in the park: "I overcharge."
In short, as the young woman who owns the antiques shop says: "Money is always a problem."

The hunt for pictures that makes up the plot of the film takes shape against this iconomic horizon. But it is not only the pictures taken or caught by the photographer Thomas that are inscribed in a network of exchanges in which they tend to gain surplus value because he overcharges for them. It is also, as we will see, the gaze itself that internalizes the rhythm, the pulsation—the *phrasing*—of the circulation of exchange. This is no doubt how we must understand the antiques dealer's retort: There are no pictures that have not already been affected by a gaze that destines them to being exchanged for other images. Or better: that makes them indebted to images to come.

In *Camera Lucida*, just after mentioning *Blow-Up* as though in passing, Barthes insists on what distinguishes cinema from photography:

> The photographic image is full, crammed: no room, nothing can be added to it. In the cinema, whose raw material is photographic, the image does not,

however, have this completeness (which is fortunate for the cinema). Why? Because the photograph, taken in flux, is impelled, ceaselessly drawn toward other views; in the cinema, no doubt, there is always a photographic referent, but this referent shifts, it does not make a claim in favor of its reality.[1]

It is quite possible, however, that *Blow-Up* makes this distinction waver, not only by showing that the photographic image is also bound to the slippages and thus to the fluctuations of exchange—even if they are slower than those of cinematic images—but also by displaying the mobility of the gaze that makes *every image* what Bresson would call an exchange value. "No absolute value of an image," Bresson said in fact, as we recall, in his *Notes on Cinematography*.[2] And this lapidary statement could hold, precisely, for the value of images in general, whether photographic or cinematographic images. Or pictorial images, for that matter (recall the fresco beneath the fresco in *Obsession*).

Let's follow Barthes's argument for a moment as he makes the *punctum* the distinctive feature of photography as opposed to cinema.

What is at issue?

Barthes first describes this *punctum* as a sort of piercing event that arises from the photograph: "A photograph's punctum is that accident which pricks me" (27). Barthes then says that this arrow that shoots out from the photo like a detail in it that pierces me, this projecting or jutting out of the photographic image, is a "supplement," a sort of addition, but an internal one: "It is what I add to the photograph and *what is nonetheless already there*" (55). Now, what is lacking in cinema is precisely the possibility of what we might call this *addition* [*appoint*] to the image:

> Do I add to the images in movies? I don't think so; I don't have time: in front of the screen, I am not free to shut my eyes; otherwise, opening them again, I would not discover the same image; I am constrained to a continuous voracity. (55)

This same iconomic gluttony inherent in cinema also robs it of the *punctum* in the second sense Barthes gives the word. Earlier in *Camera Lucida*, there is what Barthes calls "another *punctum*" (96): no longer the "detail" that makes photography poignant, but the "stigmatum" that marks it with a "that-has-been," that is, the punctiformity of the past event photography attests to "intractably," for "I can never deny that *the thing has been there*" (76), in front of the lens. Yet there again, this second *punctum*—that of referential pointing—is what is lacking in the filmic image that, we have read, doesn't have the time to "make a claim in favor of its reality" (89).

In short, if photography differs from film, it is to the extent that film doesn't give the gaze time to stop, to settle on a frame. But we have reason to ask questions of Barthes's distinction between photography and cinema, questions that *Blow-Up* constantly displays in all their forms: What is the *exposure of a gaze?* Who could ever measure its duration or stability? And what will ever guarantee that by opening our eyes again, we will find "the same image"?

Blow-Up could be described as a series of variations on the fundamental gesture of photographic capture or seizure, that is, obturation.[3] During the famous photo shoot with Veruschka (a famous model at the time who plays herself in the film), jumps in the angle of the shot, jump cuts, integrate, so to speak, the photographic interruption into the cinematographic flow. Later, during another shoot with a group of models, Thomas tells them, "Close your eyes," and he takes advantage of this to slip away, as though he were imposing a blink of the eye upon them, a blink or obturation that lasts longer than expected, that freezes into the blind waiting (it could be infinite) of a sort of game of hide-and-seek.

The longest obturation, however, comes between the moment Thomas arrives at a party at which he bumps into his friend Ron and the moment he wakes up the next morning among the leftovers, dirty dishes, and empty bottles, in an unfamiliar apartment with no one left in it. The previous evening, he told Ron about the dead body in the park, but Ron, smoking two joints at the same time, was so stoned he was in no state to hear him:

"What did you see in that park?" he asks Thomas, who resigns himself to responding laconically, "Nothing."

Thomas, who has been robbed of the photos of the park where the dead body is supposed to be, then returns to the scene of the supposed crime. We hear the wind in the leaves. He has his camera, but the dead body has disappeared. The night, the time lapse when Thomas closed his eyes and slept, was thus another long blink of the eye, a punctuation of the visible still longer than that imposed on the waiting models.

What is the time of a blink of the eye? And who will ever be able to say what might take place—or be effaced—in this gap or jump within the visible that, however, allows for the visible, makes it possible?

If *Blow-Up* thus constantly inscribes the cutting of photographic obturation into the fluidity of the cine-gaze (an obturation, then, that goes from the minute jump cuts of the opening sequence with Veruschka to Thomas's long sleep, passing by way of his hide-and-seek with the motionless models), the film also constantly introduces, by contrast, the cine-pannings of the camera-eye in the seeming fixity of the photo.

The process of photographic developing—which takes time—is thus haunted by an entirely cinematic fluidity. As background noise, we hear the tap running in the lab. Then, when Thomas, magnifying glass in hand, points or punctuates his enlarged print with a white pencil, when he traces on it a frame that he will enlarge once again, we witness the equivalent of an extremely slowed down and decomposed zoom in (an "enlarged," as it were, or "blown-up" zoom). But most of all, after Thomas has attached two enlarged photos to the wall, the camera starts panning from one to the other, goes back and forth, thus tracing a sort of ping-pong or tennis of the gaze (I will return to this).

With this back and forth of his eyes, Thomas, his index finger extended, goes from one print to the other. As though his gaze were engaged in a match (*to match*, in English, the language of the film, is to compare, to exchange terms in order to establish a comparison or equivalence between them). It is as though Thomas's vision had already been carried away in the exchange of shots that will punctuate the famous final scene of the tennis match, which we must now watch closely.

Thomas is wandering in the park. He again meets the mimes in makeup who, at the beginning of the film, crisscrossed the streets of London and now start playing a game of tennis, with neither balls nor rackets. The gazes of those who watch the game describe the back-and-forths, the to-and-fros, of the eyes exactly the same way Thomas did between the photos on his studio walls. An echo or rhyme of gazes, at a distance in the film. Then we see Thomas's own eyes make small panoramic shots (they pan, as it is sometimes put in the language of film).

What the famous final sequence of *Blow-Up* suggests, before all the interpretations that have dogged it, is thus perhaps quite simply that the gaze, insofar as it creates fictions and makes what it still doesn't see or already no longer sees, the gaze as such, even before seeing something, the pure gaze, in short, is this phrasal beat—shot and reverse shot—that is nothing other than the very form of exchange.

But an exchange that takes time. That already takes the time—however brief—of phrasing.[4]

If *Blow-Up* thus suggests that there is always already some cinema in photos, and vice versa, it is because, from the point of view of a general iconomy, the distinction between the two amounts only to a difference in the speed of exchange between images. Compared to photography, cinema of course has a certain speed in the iconic circulation through the slide changer. But even the distinctness of this contrast between the rate of circulation in the two media is diminished by what must be termed the arche-pannings of the gaze, which from the start inscribe all of visibility in an irreducible movement of exchange.

"No pictures," the antiques seller said to Thomas; "there are no pictures." No fixed or definitive image, no image that would hold absolutely, in itself. As a result, the image is always already filmic: It is (it is the image that it is) only in the context of its relation to, or exchange with, others.

But isn't this *also* what Barthes said in his own way? If we examine it more closely, wasn't Barthes's thinking of the image already, sometimes very explicitly, an iconomic thinking?

In "The Third Meaning," an essay that appeared in *Les Cahiers du Cinéma* ten years before *Camera Obscura*, Barthes characterized what must be considered the ancestor of the *punctum* in terms borrowed from the language of economics: The "obtuse meaning" (the "one too many," added like a "supplement" to the image, which bursts out "as an *accent*, the very form of an emergence") was described "as a luxury, an expenditure with no exchange."[5] And this economic register became perhaps even clearer or more obvious (if I may say so)[6] in a short 1975 article titled "Leaving the Movie Theater." Reading the following description of the mechanism of cinematographic projection, you might almost think you're hearing Deleuze and his iconomic formulation about money as the reverse of all the images of film:

> In that opaque cube, one light: the film, the screen? Yes, of course, but also (especially?), visible and unperceived, that dancing cone which pierces the darkness like a laser beam. This beam is minted, according to the rotation of its particles, into changing figures; we turn our face toward the *currency* of a gleaming vibration whose imperious jet brushes our skull.[7]

Essentially, I will perhaps have done nothing but extend this monetary or numismatic conception of film beyond cinema. With Barthes and beyond him, I have indeed attempted to understand it by "leaving the movie theater." That is, I have tried to make it hold for photography as well, and even more generally for the gaze that comes to rest [*se pose*] on any image whatsoever by immediately deposing it from its sovereign status as an image in itself.

Locations

23, rue Bénard, Paris, 75014

I recently found out that something happened near my home almost a century ago. Very close to where I live in Paris, in the fourteenth arrondissement. In a neighboring street, rue Bénard, someone upended how we think about images and their economy so profoundly that we have not yet truly taken stock of it. Someone who assessed in advance the impact of the iconomic revolution upon us.

This thinker was Walter Benjamin, who, when he was working on his essay "The Work of Art in the Age of Its Technological Reproducibility," lived at 23, rue Bénard. When I discovered this spectral proximity— spectral, for time has since dug an abyssal distance in it—when I noticed, in reading Benjamin's

correspondence from the 1930s with Horkheimer and Adorno, my first gesture, strangely, was to go to Google Maps and turn on the Street View function to see the entrance to his building. There, I saw ghosts, silhouettes,
blurred faces pass by, like on the photographs of old that Benjamin talks
about better than anyone.

Why this gesture? What was I doing in using Google Street View? I
could have (I did this later) left my apartment and gone right there.
Although this adverb, "right," isn't self-evident at a time—ours—when I
could go up to number 23, rue Bénard, by putting on glasses that would
perhaps—who knows if this will happen one day—allow me to consult
Benjamin's biography or correspondence superimposed visually upon the
real sight of the building he once lived in. In a still more vertiginous zoom,
I could have used Google Earth and zoomed in on the building from the
extraterrestrial space of the satellites that orbit us.[1]

What has happened to our gaze, then? What is this novel mobilization
that affects it?

Through Benjamin, through his concept of innervation, we can begin to
think the possibility of the strange visit with him I was able to make all the
while reading him.

Deleted Scene

The Fluctuations of the Unchained Camera (L'Herbier)

Four years after Murnau's *The Last Laugh*, Marcel L'Herbier went still further in conquering the mobility of the cine-eye in *Money* (*L'Argent*, 1928). But what he also shows is that freeing the cinematographic gaze goes hand in hand with monetizing it, with its financialization: In other words, freed of its chains, the camera is all the more bound, so to speak, to market fluctuations.

Money opens with crowd scenes at the Paris Stock Exchange,[1] with a famous high-angle shot, like a bustling anthill full of little men dressed in black, all carrying light-colored papers. It produces something like the effect of "snow," like on television screens, in days gone by, at the end of the day's programs. As though we were watching the pure wavering of the grains, of the atoms of the image.

This same wavering—the same dark silhouettes waving white papers—continues, but this time seen from closer up, when the camera takes us to

the heart of the extraordinary general assembly of the Caledonian Eagle company, at the head of which sits Nicolas Saccard, who is described as an "audacious financier, the director of the Banque Universelle, one of whose main businesses is Caledonian Eagle." Threatened by the maneuvers of his rival, Alphonse Gunderman, who is trying to bring him down, to ruin him, Saccard plans to save his Banque Universelle by financing the transatlantic flight of the aviator Jacques Hamelin.

On the one hand, money and its power, then. And on the other, the freedom of movement par excellence, this gratuitousness of flight to which L'Herbier's camera aspires (as we see in the most striking way in *Autour de L'Argent*, a "the making of" film before the fact that was made during the filming of *Money* by Jean Dréville).

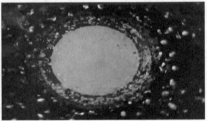

Thus, the plot can be read in part as the financialization of free movement, as its submission to monetary control, as L'Herbier describes in his extraordinary "financial chronicle" titled "Le Cinématographe et l'espace."[2] Hamelin's flight will be exactly parallel to the rise in the stock of the Banque Universelle, leading to the film's most striking juxtaposition: on the one hand, the plane's propeller as it turns, superimposed upon the round dials of his instrument panel; and on the other hand, the vertiginous whirling of the camera itself, which spins in a whirlwind above the stock exchange trading floor and describes furious circles from the dome from which it is suspended, as the camera itself seems to fly higher and higher.

Deleted Scenes

The General Fetishism of the Marxes

The short article Freud published in 1927 on fetishism is traversed by reflections on sight and visibility.[1] The first "case" mentioned is "one in which a young man had exalted a certain sort of 'shine on the nose,'" that is, in German, *Glanz auf der Nase*, which his analysis manages to retranslate into his forgotten maternal tongue, English, as a "*glance* at the nose" (152). Later, we read between the lines a debate with the French psychiatrist René Laforgue on the term *scotomization*, which names the production of a blind spot in vision.[2] Although the visible and the invisible are recurrent motifs in the text, what we should consider, nonetheless, is Freud's quasi-cinematographic description of the genesis of a fetish.

Having remarked that he risks creating "disappointment" when he describes the fetish as a "substitute [*Ersatz*] for the woman's (the mother's) penis that the little boy once believed in and—for reasons familiar to us—does not want to give up," Freud writes:

It seems . . . that when the fetish is instituted some process occurs which reminds one of the stopping of memory [*das Haltmachen der Erinnerung*] in traumatic amnesia. As in this latter case, the subject's interest comes to a halt half-way, as it were [*bleibt das Interesse wie unterwegs stehen*]; it is as though the last impression before the uncanny and traumatic one is retained as a fetish [*wird etwa der letzte Eindruck vor dem unheimlichen, traumatischen, als Fetisch festgehalten*]. Thus the foot or shoe owes its preference as a fetish—or a part of it—to the circumstance that the inquisitive boy peered at the woman's genitals from below, from her legs up [*von unten, von den Beinen her*]. (155)

The fetish, in short, is the stopping of the elevator of the gaze that climbs from floor to floor in the movement of substitution or of the metonymic exchange of impressions. The fetish arises, it is formed and stabilized, when the cinematography of general fetishism is frozen: when, in the movement of its low-angle shot, it is blocked at a certain floor of the supermarket of the visible. As Paul-Laurent Assoun puts it so well in his reading of Freud's theory, "Everything depends on the 'cinematics' of the scene and its stopping point," for the "fetish object" is essentially nothing but a "freeze-frame."[3]

We entered *The Big Store* by taking the elevator of the opening credits, adopting the rising cine-gaze that takes us through the piles of goods arranged by floors, while also stopping, regularly blocking ourselves in this same movement. If it is true that fetishism, as Freud suggests, is at once the movement of desire going from substitute to substitute and the freeze-frame that interrupts this general cinematics, we must pay special attention to the elevators that, well beyond the opening credits, constantly crisscross the department store, sliding across *The Big Store* while making its images slide.[4]

The famous chorus sung by the salespeople, led by Groucho to the frenzied rhythm of a song titled "Sing While You Sell," begins in the elevator, a figure that also seems to haunt the song lyrics ("sales will mount up to the skies," Groucho exclaims in front of the employees in transport). Later, in the hilarious scene that begins with the arrival of a large Italian family, the father, following Groucho's advice, pushes a button and so makes a four-story bed rise up like an elevator; it contains Harpo and Chico, who go past as though they were stuck in the frames of a piece of film. In this same scene, playing the elevator-bed control panel like a virtuoso, Harpo makes the beds go up and down, as though he were the conductor of the general elevatorality of film. Finally, just before the denouement of the happy ending, in the long sequence in which the store manager chases the three Marx brothers, the elevator explicitly becomes the place where the capture of the image, that is, the arrest of its circulation, is played out. What the manager tries to recuperate, and what the Marx brothers try to keep, is the photo that stands as proof of the plot against Tommy, the heir of the department store. And this compromising photogram passes from one hand to another, from floor to floor.

The elevator, as we see, is the equipment, the mechanism, that animates the supermarket of general fetishism: On the one hand, it maintains the

continuous scrolling of images, makes possible the circulation of exchanges and substitutions without which film could not exist; but on the other hand, it is also striated— frame by frame—which is to say that it already bears the mark of all the freeze-frames in which our gaze, captured, will be fixed.

Deleted Scenes

The Amortization of the Gaze (*King Kong*)

King Kong is a film about making a film, to be sure. But it is also a film about cinema as the monetization and commodification of seeing.

Very quickly we embark on what would have to be called the *moving picture ship*, as the very first exchange in the original version directed by Merian C. Cooper and Ernest B. Schoedsack in 1933 puts it: "Say, is this the moving picture ship?" asks a man who, on the Hoboken docks, with Manhattan skyscrapers in the background, passes a night watchman making his rounds along a docked boat. The name of the ship is *Venture*: adventure, enterprise. As in *venture capital*, the money invested in innovations, where the profits, like the losses, can be considerable. The man preparing to raise the anchor, the director Carl Denham (Robert Armstrong), soon declares, "Listen, I'm going out to make the greatest picture in the world."

Let's get on board the moving picture ship with him and open our eyes wide to try to see what happens to them, to sights and points of view that are exchanged in being monetized. Among the countless ways in which *King Kong* can be interpreted (Adorno saw in it the totalitarian state; Virginie Despentes reads in it a "chaos prior to genre" without "cock, or balls, or breasts"; for others what is at stake in it is at once feminist and postcolonial), what I am concerned with here is this economy of gazes.[1]

The filmmaker, Carl, takes a young unemployed actress, Ann Darrow (Fay Wray), on his film expedition, whose exact destination is unknown to us, as it is to the crew of the *Venture*. Once the ship is at sea, he embarks on a series of screen tests with her in front of the camera. He guides her acting while filming; he directs; he leads her eyes with his words, so that Ann's gaze is broken down, articulated, accentuated, punctuated in each of its micromovements:

"Look up slowly, Ann. That's it. You don't see anything. Now look higher. Still higher. Now you see him. You're amazed. You can't believe it. Your eyes open wider. It's horrible, Ann, but you can't look away."

At the end, Ann screams, as Carl asks her to do, while covering her eyes. But she hasn't seen anything yet, no more than have Carl himself, the captain, or the mate, who comments, "What does he think she's really going to see?" What we have just witnessed is thus a graduation of the gaze, but one that precedes the object of this gaze. Carl in fact told Ann this, before starting to film: "You're quite calm. You don't expect to see a thing. Then you just follow my directions." It is as though for Ann there was nothing but a prepunctuated scale of visual values or magnitudes, an optical route measured out in advance that her gaze has to fit itself to, adopting one after the other the points of view that are prescribed for it, that await it.

It is thus Ann's gaze that is punctuated. And the punctuating gaze, Carl's, the gaze of the filmmaker who seems to have the privilege of measuring, calculating, distributing, and allotting the values of the other gazes—this gaze remains largely offscreen.

In the 2005 remake directed by Peter Jackson, we only come to the moving picture ship after a long prelude. Carl (Jack Black) has managed to convince Ann (Naomi Watts) to play the leading role in his film, and we head out with them to the port. Getting out of the taxi, dazzled by the size of the ship, this time *she* asks, "Is this the moving picture ship?" No, it's the little boat to the side, Carl tells her. The real magnitude, or even excess, will only enter the scene later, with the eponymous character, King Kong himself, the metonym for the film in which he appears and to which he gives his name, a part for the whole that could well exceed the whole of which it is a part.

What happens, then, when the gazes of this or that character encounter immensity, that which is beyond measure, what cannot be calculated?

In the 1933 *King Kong*, as special effects techniques of the time would have it, Kong appears to Ann, who is tied to the altar as an offering or human sacrifice, by means of a rear projection screen. And it seems that, during the filming, the actress who played Ann, Fay Wray, found herself in the same situation as her character doing screen tests with Carl on the ship's deck. For, too close to the screen on which the giant gorilla was projected, she saw nothing and had to trust the director's instructions to scream at the right moment.[2]

But the fact remains that, alternating between the shots and reverse angle shots that punctuate the first face-to-face between Ann and Kong, we never

gaze with the latter's eyes. We see Ann look up, higher than the camera, and the shot thus literally places us *under* the monster's point of view.

This vertical triangulation of points of view—Kong above us, and us facing Ann—is in a sense the very interval between, on the one hand, the system of exchanges of gaze (alternating between us and Ann) and, on the other hand, the unexchangeable, the point of view of what remains outside this circuit (Kong). Kong is outside the circulation of points of view, as though his perspective had no equivalent.

There is no exchange of looks as Ann is carried away by the beast in the 2005 *King Kong*, any more than there is the 1933 version. Between Ann and the beast, the symmetrical shot-reverse angle shot is in fact carefully avoided thanks to a surprising series of substitutions: We see Ann with eyes that are not Kong's (the point of view is too low and close to her to be his); and, every time we expect to look into Kong's eyes from Ann's point of view, we are given a different viewpoint. First, the gazeless gaze of the Indigenous peoples, the worshippers in this sacrificial ceremony who, their eyes rolled back in a trance, seem precisely no longer to have eyes with which to see. Then the panicked eyes of Jack Driscoll (Adrien Brody) and of the crew of the *Venture*, who have gone in search of Ann.

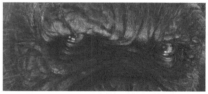

We have to wait, after Ann's heartrending cry, until Carl approaches the wall cautiously for the long-deferred reverse angle shot finally to arrive. The exchange of looks finally takes place, not between Kong and Ann, but between the monster and the filmmaker. And in the form of the beast's unforgettable gaze at the camera.

To understand the economy of this gaze, we have to back up a bit. We have to remember how it was constantly anticipated, on Skull Island, by things that seemed to look in advance at the people who discovered them.

To recall: The moving picture ship, as though it had arrived by accident at its destination, is shipwrecked on a rock that is also and above all an eye. The shot-reverse angle shot between Carl and the monster was therefore anticipated in the filmic venture coming aground against a stony gaze that literally predicted Kong's gaze.

We could of course interpret this gaze—the gaze that looks at us from the side of things—in terms of Lacan's discussion of the objet a in the field of the scopic, in the domain of what he called "seeingness [*voyure*]." Carl could then say, like Lacan, "On the side of things, there is the gaze, that is to say, things look at me."[3] But what we should be more concerned with here is that the moving picture ship obviously seems to find, with this gaze, something like a point of abutment, a limit at which its journey [*cours*]

comes to an end [*en bout de course*]. The eye it comes across is thus the terminal point, the end to which the cinematographic voyage of the *Venture* has carried us.

And it is thus also its beginning—perhaps better, its *principle*—for it is from the moving picture ship stalled by the stability of a gaze that is immovable and apparently as solid as a rock that Carl goes off to explore the unknown island. He sets out in a rowboat with his small team and his camera. And we then see that there are in fact countless impassable and threatening rocks surrounding the beginning of the filming. It turns out, then, that Skull Island, on which the moving picture ship has come aground, is not simply the gaze of one capital Eye: This Eye turns out to be plural; it has already been minted into a whirl of multiplied gazes among which the camera circulates, at once looking and looked at.

I have said that Kong's gaze, this gaze of the Thing, the most terrifying gaze there is, dominates all the other gazes from a point of view that, it seems, cannot be assessed and that is without equivalent. But the whole issue for the film is precisely to make it too enter into an exchange of looks. It is a question of monetizing it, of multiplying it to inscribe it in a calculable, measurable, cost-effective economy of profit. *King Kong* is essentially the story of scopic immoderation that is moderated, the story of the domestication by the market of an exorbitant sight.

This is why Carl throws his bottle of chloroform into Kong's eyes, which then seem to smoke as they give off numbing steam. And just after having made the eyes of the Thing close, the director exclaims, "The whole world will pay to see this. We're millionaires, boys." The gaze of the Thing has been *amortized*, in both senses of the word: It has been rendered as though dead [*mort*] and made profitable in advance by the use that will be made of it.

Formats

Surplus Definition (*Redacted*)

Today more than ever, the value of images is embedded in their resolution. When the resolution is low, when the images are "poor," as Hito Steyerl writes, they circulate more quickly: Their qualitative impoverishment makes it easier to disseminate them.[1] But the speed with which images spread or are exchanged is only the most superficial, the most immediately obvious, aspect of what we might call the iconomy of formats. In the digital age, many other transactions take place imperceptibly *under the surface* of images, that is, in their very texture, in the text of their code.

Jonathan Sterne has put forward a "theory of format" that, although it is formulated for sound, suggests by analogy how the economy is already at work within the image. This is what he has to say about the MP3 format that has conquered the sound market, making itself inescapable there:

MP3s are so plentiful because they are so small. They use considerably less bandwidth and storage space than the .wav files one finds on standard compact discs. To make an MP3, a program called an encoder takes a .wav file (or some other audio format) and compares it to a mathematical model of the gaps in human hearing. . . . It discards the parts of the audio signal that are unlikely to be audible. . . . The technique of removing redundant data in a file is called *compression*. The technique of using a model of a listener to remove additional data is a special kind of "lossy" compression called *perceptual coding.*[2]

There is something in this of an internal difference between sound as it is written and as it is heard: The encoded sound discards aspects of the signal that our human mechanisms of perception cannot detect (this is why one speaks of the "loss" of content that takes place in compression). And with this inaudible gap can be created what Sterne calls "surplus definition," which he is clearly thinking in terms of surplus value: If a system of coding, taking advantage of the gaps in our perception, can make do with less definition than the media channel transporting the information allows for, if it thus creates lighter files and thus frees up room for others to circulate, then this residual space can become a sort of economic profit. It can be exploited, Sterne says, in the form of "perceptual capital" that corresponds to the "accumulated value generated by a surplus definition" (48).

The space in which surplus value (Marx's *Mehrwert*) is created is thus the gap between different formattings of the same sound or image. It is the difference between high and low definition *insofar as this difference is not perceived as such*, insofar as it remains invisible or inaudible. As a result, Sterne quite rightly notes that perceptual capital could just as well be called "imperceptual capital," since it profits from "material that users do not perceive" (48).

There are of course processes and models of compression that are specific to the visible. I won't go into the details of them here: Within a fixed image a color zone can be digitized, for example, by leaving out the micro-contrasts it contains and which the eye cannot detect; in the case of moving images, encoding techniques can be used that retain only the change from one image to the next. In short, as with sound, a whole economic potential of savings and profits is held in reserve—hidden, encrypted—under the surface of coded images. But in the new iconomy that is configured thus, the source of potential surplus value inherent in the digital texture of the image cannot be separated from what happens with regard to its *fiduciary value*, that is, from the faith or confidence (*fiducia*, in Latin) we have in it.

What does this mean?

We have to go a step further here, further than Sterne's theory of format. For the very possibility of (im)perceptual capital is inscribed in the field of what we might call a *general steganography*. In the common sense, steganography (from the Greek *steganos*: "opaque," "thick," "covering") is the hiding of secret messages in the digital encoding of texts, images, or sounds. Pieces of information can thus be concealed in the countless lines of code that define what we will read, see, or hear: No one will notice them (it in fact often happens that one image is hidden within another, for example).[3] Now, in this same way, in the case of lossy compression that generates surplus definition, everything superfluous is deleted from the code: Kilo- or megabytes are won by introducing holes, inaudible or invisible gaps in the digital text, so that the (im)perceptual capital is also a form of steganography, except that it is inverted, since it consists in recoding in order to remove, rather than add, information. In both cases, there is a hidden writing or rewriting: The iconomic capital the images carry in that they can be reformatted goes hand in hand with the possibility that they have secret gray zones, that they don't look like what they really are or do.

In short, the era—*our* era—in which profitability is already at stake in every pixel of an image is also the era in which the smallest parts composing the same image can be manipulated: The capitalization of perception, as it is inscribed in how formats are managed, is inseparable from the fluctuations of what we might call the *trust capital* of the visible (the French expression *capital-confiance* is used in the language of marketing to indicate how well known a product becomes among consumers for being reliable).

These are the issues that *Redacted*, Brian De Palma's 2007 film, presents in its own—masterful—way, not only because it shows the exchanges between different visual formats in circulation in the global iconomic space today, but because it also suggests that the encoding of these formats affects the *truth value* of images.

We of course tend to judge or prejudge the credibility of an image solely on the basis of how high or low its definition is: Generally, we think that a "poor" image, for example, one taken with a cell phone, has greater testimonial value because it was taken with a cheap and common technology that allows us to get close to the scene of action, to blend in without attracting attention. Rightly or wrongly, the "poor" image thus passes as the most direct of direct images, those from gonzo, undercover journalism, or even passersby, rather than those from media outlets or reports. This is also the case, in *Redacted*, of the green images filmed with night vision by an embedded journalist, one the army allows in the field with soldiers. At the other end of the spectrum, on the side of high quality images, is what De Palma himself describes as a "fake French documentary" filmed at the checkpoint where soldiers are stationed: With its glossy images and elegant soundtrack, at times borrowed from *Barry Lyndon*, one might, on first seeing it, believe it is a mock-documentary rather than a testimonial worthy of the name.[4]

But *Redacted* does not—or does not only—speak of this truth value when, even before the opening credits, even before there are any images properly speaking, the film presents us with a warning before the fact:

> This film is entirely fiction, inspired by an incident widely reported to have occurred in Iraq. While some of the events depicted here may resemble those of the reported incident, the characters are entirely fictional, and their words and actions should not be confused with those of real persons.

How are we to decipher this warning? Or rather, how does the film offer it for us to read? How does it prescribe in advance our reading of it?

We know from eye tracking studies that reading a text always involves quick saccades. The gaze does not move from one word to the next, but engages in much more irregular punctuations; it jumps syntagms, entire blocks, to go sound out, to hit upon, some later point in the sentence, paragraph, or page. In short, the reader's eyes are always ahead of themselves and never stop bouncing around.

This is also how we read the warning the film presents us with, but the saccades of our gaze are not limited, here, to anticipating what we have not yet read even as we already glimpse it: They also seem endowed with the strange power of blacking out words. For this text is redacted in the very time allotted for its reading. We have barely begun to read the beginning when it is erased before our eyes: The word *fiction* is crossed out. We try to continue reading, but what follows is also erased before our

very eyes: The adjective *fictional* is blacked out. And we no longer know where to look. The verb *may* disappears, followed by the past participle *confused*, and so forth. The time of reading seems to coincide vertiginously with the time of the erasure it struggles against. And it is therefore as though each glance to try and see were immediately doubled by a blanking that is indissociable from it.

Why am I emphasizing thus what is written on the screen before the very first image? Why pause, before we've even begun to see anything at all, over this rewriting, this encoding that obscures and that, it seems, always goes along with or inhabits the slightest saccades of our gaze?

Much later in the film, we find the same erasures or deletions censuring different zones of text on an internet page, which also contains blurry images as well as the video of a masked soldier testifying about how American soldiers in his squad raped a young Iraqi girl before assassinating her:

> I am making this video to expose a situation that happened to my squad and that I think people should know about. I'm hiding my identity from the public because I'm afraid the FBI and the Department of Defense and even the insurgents can trace my ID and find me. They already got one of my guys, and I'm not going to take any chances. But this needs to be said. For legal reasons and for my personal safety, I cannot reveal the time or the place or the soldiers involved, but believe me, everything I'm about to tell you, everything, is absolutely true.

Redacted, as De Palma has explained in numerous interviews, constantly copies, mimics, the texture of images that circulate on the web, like the page that contains the video of this testimony. "All the images in my film," the filmmaker confided on the site lesinrocks.com (September 18, 2007), "are replicas of others that can be seen on the internet." And he added, "Look up 'soldiers in Iraq,' 'rape,' 'murder,' on Youtube and you'll find everything. . . . Using a digital camera stood to reason; all the images of this war and all the imaginable sources of information on the subject *are* the product of going digital." Cinema does not make these found images "in its own name," then, as Emmanuel Burdeau emphasized after the film was released, but takes them "from an archive of which the internet is both the reality and the metaphor."[5]

Thus, we see numerous webpages in Arabic on which the soldiers filming—especially private first class Angel Salazar (Izzy Diaz), the director of a sort of war journal on MiniDV—are themselves filmed by Iraqis. And the passage from one type of image to another is marked, punctuated, by various forms of wipe that become the very sign of the change in format. Later, when one of the soldiers is blown up by a mine, we even see three different formats one after the other: the shooting of the scene by Angel filming with the MiniDV, then the repetition of the same scene posted on the web by the rebels who planted the mine, and finally surveillance images taken by the security camera at the military camp, where the soldiers are fed up with awaiting the worst.

It would seem, then, that cinema "has fallen to second place in the order of images," as Emmanuel Burdeau writes, that it "organizes their distribution," but that none of them belong to it properly speaking. In short, it has only "usufruct."[6]

Yet among the images that are found, gleaned here and there, and edited with wipes that constantly emphasize the difference in their format, the webpage of the hooded soldier's testimony has a particular status. Let's look more closely at the inscriptions, the traces, it carries. Where, in what space, are these black censor bars and this blurring found? The erasures obviously don't cross out or redact the page of the site itself (one doesn't rewrite *right on* an internet page, one re-encodes it). The strike-throughs are thus not

found *on* the page that is shown, but rather *between* it and what we see. And the same goes for the blurriness of the fuzzy part of the screen.

What does this mean?

It is as though the occult work of formatting—this secret economy that, beneath the surface of images, calculates the profitability of the imperceptible—is here shown in broad daylight. The difference in formats or image resolution, we have seen, is in fact nothing other than the degree of their *internal* erasure or blurring, without us noticing it: What is at stake is in a sense an (im)perceptible steganography. And so we can say that De Palma's film does not content itself with showing how differently formatted images of the same event mix or follow one another in the global network. It does not merely display their coexistence by punctuating their disparity with wipes. With the image of a website that is *visibly* rewritten and blurry, the director goes further and shows the stratification of differences in format *in the very thickness of the image*: Blurriness is added to or superimposed on a photo that was itself no doubt already compressed or pixelated, just as erasure operates on words that themselves have no doubt already passed through the filter of censorship. In short, it is as though steganographic reencoding were raised to the level of the visible or readable, as though it came to the surface and appeared as such (which, strangely, almost amounts to producing a sort of *depth in the field of format*).

Let's go back to just before the opening credits where, as you recall, we were given a written warning about the fictionality of the images while our reading was made indissociable from an erasure that doubles each of the

 saccades of our eyes. A few letters rise up from this redacting and deleting that opens the film, letters that, enlarged and detached from the crossed-out words, are recombined to outline the title: *r e d a ct e d*. And this title immediately becomes the subject of a sentence displayed on screen: "*r e d a c t e d* visually documents imagined events before, during and after a 2006 rape and murder in Samarra."

You will no doubt ask: How can a fiction be documented? And especially, how is the promise to do so linked to the first images properly speaking, on which is immediately displayed the title of this "war diary" filmed on MiniDV by private first class Angel Salazar: *Tell Me No Lies?*

These are not new questions. They have been asked many times, especially by all the hybrid forms between documentary and fiction that tend to be classified, after a fashion, under a variety of names, including "mockumentary," *documenteur* (the portmanteau Agnès Varda used as a title in 1981), and "docudrama." De Palma himself knows this, and in an interview with rottentomatoes.com speaks of his film as a "fragmented mockdocumentary."

But above and beyond these rather hackneyed considerations of the rhetoric of truth and fiction, of the truth of fiction and the fiction of truth, this sequence before the credits also points to something else. By having its title emerge from a text that is read *at the same time* that it is encrypted and erased, the film seems to want to show that, in the era of general steganography, the value of the image, its fiduciary as well as perceptual capital, consists in the secret writing of its very coming into appearance.

CREDITS

Thank you:

To my friends in Sydney, Dimitris Vardoulakis, Amanda Third, and Chris Peterson, who were incomparably generous hosts;

To my students in the seminar "Economies of the Visual" at Brown University—especially Nathan Lee, David Mullins, and Tyler Theus—who accompanied me in my iconomic explorations;

To Emmanuel Burdeau and Raymond Bellour, who, one October day in 2013, in response to my questions, improvised a fascinating dialogue on the filmography of elevators;

To Érik Bullot, who invited me to write, in two voices or with four hands, a reading of certain scenes of the Marx brothers (our conspired duo appeared in *Trafic* 90 [2014]);

To Antonio Somaini, who opened my eyes to what is at stake in the resolution of images (my remarks on *Redacted* were first presented at the conference *Haute et basse définition*, which he organized in October 2013);

To François Quintin, who, when in October 2013 he entrusted me with presenting a seminar on the future Lafayette Foundation and its space, designed by Rem Koolhaas, led me into the unexpected world of escalators;

To Dork Zabunyan and Elsa Boyer, in remembrance of our beautiful discussions of oculometry on the occasion of a seminar in Lille, on December 18, 2014;

To Yves Citton, who provided a venue for a first sketch of iconomy in *Multitudes* 57 (2014);

To Laura Odello, who led me to *Alfred Hitchcock Presents*, who elicited the pages on *King Kong* and *Godzilla* (they were first published in her *Blockbuster* at Prairies ordinaires in 2013), who shares my nocturnal viewings . . .

1. In a certain manner, the reader of *Hits: Philosophy in the Jukebox*, trans. Will Bishop (New York: Fordham University Press, 2011) was invited to move within the supermarket of the audible in order to explore what I then called "capital's intimate hymn" (57), which rises from the ground of a "homology between the market and the psyche" (65).

2. In a remarkable article, Erik Dussere shows how, from *Double Indemnity* (Billy Wilder, 1944) to *Fight Club* (David Fincher, 1999), the supermarket is not merely one filmic place among others but is generalized into an "endless supermarket." Dussere, "Out of the Past, Into the Supermarket," *Film Quarterly* 60, no. 1 (2006): 24.

3. Karl Marx, *Zur Kritik der politischen Ökonomie*, in *Werke* (Berlin: Dietz Verlag, 1968), 13:8–9. *Collected Works of Karl Marx and Frederick Engels* (London: Lawrence & Wishart, 1975), 29:263.

4. Karl Marx and Friedrich Engels, *Ökonomisch-philosophische Manuskripte aus dem Jahre 1844*, in *Werke*, 40:540. *Collected Works*, 3:300.

5. Marx, *Ökonomisch-philosophische Manuskripte*, 540. *Collected Works*, 3:301–2. [The English translation has been lightly modified to follow the author's French.—Trans.]

6. See Jacques Rancière, *The Politics of Aesthetics: The Distribution of the Sensible* (London: Continuum, 2004).

7. See Marie-José Mondzain, *Image, Icon, Economy: The Byzantine Origins of the Contemporary Imaginary*, trans. Rico Franses (Stanford, Calif.: Stanford University Press, 2005), 123. Citing and commenting upon Mondzain's book, Susan Buck-Morss uses the word *iconomy* once and the word *iconomics* twice. Buck-Morss, "Visual Empire," *Diacritics* 37, no. 2–3 (2008): 183, 185. Davide Panagia proposes the term *iconomy* to name "a space of image production and

circulation," that is "mind," in Hume. Panagia, *Impressions of Hume: Cinematic Thinking and the Politics of Discontinuity* (Lanham, Md.: Rowman and Little-field, 2013), 84. In a wonderful study of the "state of exception" of the image, Emmanuel Alloa speaks of *Ikonomia*. See "Oikonomia: Der Ausnahmezustand des Bildes und seine byzantinische Begründung," in *Bild-Ökonomie: Haush-alten mit Sichtbarkeiten*, ed. Emmanuel Alloa and Francesca Falk (Paperborn: Wilhelm Fink, 2013), 310.

8. For the "rule" (*horos*) decreed by the Council of Hieria, see Mondzain's excellent presentation and translation in "L'image mensongère," *Rue Descartes*, 8–9 (November 1993): 20. On economy as incarnation, see also Giorgio Agamben's remarks in *The Kingdom and the Glory: For a Theological Genealogy of Economy and Government*, trans. Lorenzo Chiesa (with Matteo Mandarini) (Stanford, Calif.: Stanford University Press, 2011), 61–62.

9. See Aden Kumler's remarkable article "The Multiplication of the Spe-cies: Eucharistic Morphology in the Middle Ages," *RES: Anthropology and Aes-thetics*, 59–60 (2011): 187–88. The Latin expression *in modum denarii* is found, for example, in Honorius Augustodunensis's *Eucharistion* (twelfth century) and in Guillaume Durand's *Rationale Divinorum Officiorum* (around 1286).

10. Gilles Deleuze, *Cinema 2: The Time-Image*, trans. Hugh Tomlinson and Robert Galeta (Minneapolis: University of Minnesota Press, 1989), 77 (my emphasis). Translation modified.

11. Gilles Deleuze, *Cinema 1: The Movement-Image*, trans. Hugh Tomlin-son and Barbara Habberjam (Minneapolis: University of Minnesota, 1986), 59. As Jacques Rancière puts it very nicely, "Cinema is not the name of an art. It is the name of the world." Rancière, "From One Image to Another? Deleuze and the Ages of Cinema," in *Film Fables*, trans. Emiliano Battista (London: Berg, 2006), 109. One could find in Jean-Luc Nancy a slightly more restricted version of the same statement, namely, that cinema is an "existen-tial," that is, "a condition of possibility of existing." Jean-Luc Nancy, "Cinéfile et cinémonde," *Trafic* 50 (2004): 183–90. I myself have proposed, in *Apocalypse-Cinema: 2012 and Other Ends of the World*, trans. Will Bishop (New York: Fordham University Press, 2015), to take up and appropriate a famous (too famous) phrase from Derrida—"il n'y a pas de hors-texte" ["there is no outside text"]—to describe the arche-filmic structure and experience of the world. *Il n'y a pas de hors-film* [there is nothing outside the film], I said, then, because the real with which one might wish to oppose cinema itself already has the structure of cinema (117). In *Technics and Time, 3: Cinematic Time and the Ques-tion of Malaise*, trans. Stephen Francis Barker (Stanford, Calif.: Stanford Uni-versity Press, 2011), Bernard Stiegler uses the term "arche-cinema" to name "the cinema of consciousness," that is, consciousness *as* cinema (6, 35).

12. I transcribe his monologue literally. The idea that a film is its own accounting is essentially a variation on a remark often attributed to

Godard—but which is perhaps apocryphal—that is, that "a film should always be the documentary of its own filming" (quoted by Raymond Bellour in *L'Entre-images: Photo, cinema, video* [Paris: La Différence, 1990], 1:148). Alain Bergala attributes this remark to Rossellini: "Rossellini was no doubt the first cineaste who was convinced that, whatever one does, however much one might want to invent a fiction, a film is always the documentary of its own filming." See Bergala, "Roberto Rossellini et l'invention du cinéma moderne," preface to Roberto Rossellini, *Le Cinéma révélé* (Paris: Éditions de l'Étoile, 1984), 27.

13. Walter Benjamin, "Das Kunstwerk im Zeitalter seiner technischen Reproduzierbarkeit," in *Gesammelte Schriften*, ed. Rolf Tiedemann and Hermann Schweppenhäuser (Frankfurt-am-Main: Suhrkamp, 1974), 1:442. "The Work of Art in the Age of Its Technological Reproducibility," in *Walter Benjamin: Selected Writings Volume 3*, ed. Howard Eiland and Michael W. Jennings (Cambridge, Mass.: Harvard University Press, 2002), 123. In the version of the essay translated in the Harvard edition, the second version, the quote is found in the eighth footnote. In the German edition of Benjamin quoted by the author, it forms part of the fifth thesis.—Trans.

14. On the presence of advertisements in films, see Chantal Douchet, "Cinéma et publicité: Le Droit d'asile," in *Le Cinéma et l'argent*, ed. Laurent Creton (Paris: Nathan, 1999): "Direct financing is generally designated by the term 'product placements.' These allow for advertising to be an integral part of the film and to be hidden in order to be more apparent" (90). Contrary to what one might think, the connections between cinema and advertising are not a recent evolution (88). "We should not forget that the first Lumière films were often nothing more than 'ads': from their very first film, *Sortie d'usine*, which was meant to extol the photographic plates of the Maison Lumière, to the film on Sunlight bars of soap, called *Le Défilé du huitième bataillon de Lausanne*, passing by way of the films titled *Débarquement/Embarquement* produced for Evian mineral water, etc." The following example gives us an idea of how so-called "product placements" function: "The [Swiss] agency Propaganda conducted . . . an impact study, in 1995, concerning *Regarding Henry* (Mike Nichols, 1991). In this film, with Harrison Ford in the title role, several brands appear as 'product placements,' notably Ajax . . . , Ritz . . . , Merit. . . . Of the one hundred and twenty people surveyed immediately upon exiting the theatre, . . . the scores turned out to be very high. . . . Now, for an international film like this, the charge for a product placement varies between 30,000 and 50,000 dollars, depending upon frequency and visibility" (97–98). See, in this same book, the chapter by François Garçon on insurance in the film industry ("Du risque de fabrication dans l'industrie cinématographique: La Garantie de bonne fin"): Godard could have based a remake of *All's Well* on this. The bank demands from the producer a "third-party guarantee" in the form of a "performance

guarantee." The "guarantee company" must ensure, in particular, "the delivery of the film on the date indicated in the distribution contracts" (the bank advances the producer the profits anticipated from those distribution contracts) and "the reimbursement of the credit given the producer, should the film be abandoned or not accepted by the distributer for legally valid reasons, such as a delay in delivery" (80). The guarantor then has permanent control; "each week" he must receive "a detailed financial statement with a precise explanation of all the items that have been modified in relation to the agreed upon budget" (81), and he even gets a so-called takeover clause that allows him to replace a delinquent producer. But this guarantee must be guaranteed in turn: "The performance guarantee is charged at a flat rate. The cost of the performance guarantee is . . . 3% of the total budget. The guarantor does not hold the entire premium. To cover the risk, he must buy insurance from companies with the necessary means. Thus, most companies that offer performance guarantees are themselves insured by Lloyd's on the London market" (84).

15. After hearing this lecture, Chris Fleming sent me the following clarification in an email on May 7, 2014: "The stickers on the fridge—as banal as they may seem—are . . . slogans of Alcoholics Anonymous. . . . AA makes a great point of counting time: . . . members are usually very aware of their 'clean time,' right down to the exact day."

16. "World Destruction," by DJ Afrika Bambaata's group Time Zone, vocals by John Lydon, the former singer for the Sex Pistols.

17. Hervé Aubron has offered a beautiful analysis of this opening gesture that is also, immediately, a closure: "*L'Argent* opens by closing. At least, it opens on a closure: that, in a close-up, of an ATM whose metal panel slides to seal it like a vault. . . . First, then, this fugitive gap of the ATM, which must be closed off quickly so that the film can start. The closing and sealing of the panel reestablish a unified ground, allowing it to accommodate figures: on the brushed metal sheet headlights are reflected and, most of all, the opening credits are inscribed. . . . Perhaps there is an ATM, simply occulted, behind every ground, every shot of the film that begins." But why limit in historical terms this relationship between the film image and the money that would be its other side? Why date the question thus ("is every shot in a film, *in 1983*, a counterfeit bill?" [my emphasis]), why make it into a simple expression of something in the air at the time?: "Bresson fears that no shot, *in the 1980s*, can escape the commerce of images" (my emphasis). Why confine thus the scope of the initial double exposure (money hidden away behind images) to a "decade of implosion"—the 1980s—however singular it might be? See "Bresson à l'heure du dépôt de bilan," *Vertigo* 44 (Autumn 2012): 54–55.

18. The French *coupure* is at once a cut, as in the process of editing a film, and a banknote.—Trans.

19. As Jonathan Beller notes, "Price, then, appears as a proto-image" (58). Or again: "Price, therefore, is a proto-image, the image of the object's exchange-value" (77). In Beller, *The Cinematic Mode of Production: Attention Economy and the Society of the Spectacle* (Hanover, N.H.: Dartmouth College Press, 2012). In "The Work of Art in the Age of Its Technological Reproducibility," Walter Benjamin already emphasized that "bronzes, terra cottas, and coins were the only art works [the Greeks] could produce in large numbers" (252). In the remarkable posthumous fragment titled "Capitalism as Religion," he even proposed a sort of program of study: "A comparison between the images of the saints [*Heiligenbildern*] of the various religions and the banknotes of different states. The spirit that speaks from the ornamental design [*Ornamentik*] of banknotes." *Gesammelte Schriften* VI, 102. *Selected Writings, Volume 1: 1913–1926*, ed. Marcus Bullock and Michael W. Jennings (Cambridge, Mass.: Harvard University Press, 2004), 290.

20. See Robert Bresson, *Notes on Cinematography*, trans. Jonathan Griffin (New York: Urizen Books, 1977): "If an image, looked at by itself, expresses something sharply, if it involves an interpretation, it will not be transformed on contact with other images. The other images will have no power over it, and it will have no power over the other images. Neither action, nor reaction. It is definitive and unusable in the cinematographer's system. . . . Flatten my images (as if ironing them), *without attenuating them*" (5). We find this same demand in several interviews: "I have noticed that the flatter an image is, the less it expresses, the more it will transform when it comes into contact with other images." "A Film Made of Hands, Objects, and Glances," in *Bresson on Bresson: Interviews, 1943–1983* (New York: New York Review Books, 2016), 23. And again: "I don't like to talk about technique, largely because I don't believe in technique, but let's say that my obsession for flattening images has a good reason behind it. I believe, in fact I am certain . . . that if an image remains the same, isolated on the screen, and doesn't change when you put it next to another image, there is no transformation, there is no cinematography." In Robert Bresson et al., "To Create Life without Copying It," in *Bresson on Bresson*, 368.

21. The French *passe-vues* refers to a mechanism, similar to the magic lantern, that allows for the changing of images. See Szendy's treatment in "*Deleted Scenes*: Doors and Slide Changers in *Pickpocket* and *Obsession*," in this volume.—Trans.

22. The word *infra-mince* designates an infinite smallness and comes from Duchamp, who used it to describe the (nearly) imperceptible difference between objects.—Trans.

23. Bresson et al., "To Create Life without Copying It," 105.

24. Bresson, *Notes on Cinematography*, 5. If the cinematographic as such resides for Bresson precisely in the exchange value of images, we could say,

with Pierre Gabaston, that "the pickpocket is the cinematographer." See Gabaston, *Pickpocket de Robert Bresson* (Crisnée: Yellow Now, 1990), 39. Gabaston quite correctly suggests that "the pickpocket (the cinematographer), the voyeur/voyager in the subway . . . steals from the visible" (65).

25. Deleuze, *Time-Image*, 77. Benjamin Franklin gives this expression its canonical formulation. It punctuates his *Advice to a Young Tradesman*, written in 1748, which Max Weber read as a document in which "the spirit of capitalism" was expressed in its "almost classical purity." See Weber, *The Protestant Ethic and the Spirit of Capitalism*, trans. Anthony Giddens (London: Routledge, 1992), 14. It is nevertheless difficult to assign the phrase a precise origin. We can recognize it in Theophrastus of Eresos (fourth century BC) as cited by Diogenes Laërtius in his *Lives and Opinions of Eminent Philosophers*: "Of all expenditures, the most costly is time" (*poluteles analōma einai ton khronon*). In Henri Bergson's *Creative Evolution*, we find what looks like a remarkable variation on Franklin's formulation. It appears in a passage Deleuze very clearly alludes to at the very beginning of *Time-Movement*, when he speaks of the "cinematographic illusion" according to Bergson, that is, the idea that one can reconstruct true movement, becoming, with immobile cuts to which are added an "impersonal, abstract movement," that is, the movement that is "'in' the apparatus" (1). Bergson identifies this illusion through the "philosophy of Ideas" that developed "from Plato to Plotinus": The Idea (*eidos*, in Greek) is "the stable view taken of the instability of things," such that "to reduce things to Ideas is therefore to resolve becoming into its principal moments, each of these being, moreover, by the hypothesis, screened from the laws of time and, as it were, plucked out of eternity" (342). Three pages later, Bergson concludes that the so-called "philosophy of Ideas," for which the "reality" of time is eternity rather than becoming, would from then on have thought time according to the logic of a debt that cannot be repaid: "The philosophy of . . . ideas . . . establishes between eternity and time the same relation as between a piece of gold and the small change—change so small that payment goes on forever without the debt being paid off. The debt could be paid at once with the piece of gold" (345). Henri Bergson, *Creative Evolution*, trans. Arthur Mitchell (New York: Modern Library, 1944). Formulating the iconomic equivalence with which we are concerned (image = money) and superimposing that of the capitalist dictum passed on by Franklin (money = time), Deleuze could well also be remembering this passage from Bergson, without citing it explicitly. Accordingly, as we will see immediately, the question of debt is crucial in the Deleuzian iconomy.

26. Henri Bergson, "Memory of the Present and False Recognition," in *Mind-Energy: Lectures and Essays*, trans. H. Wildon Carr (London: Macmillan, 1920), 160–61.

27. Karl Marx, *Capital*, I, chapter 4. *Das Kapital*, in *Werke* (Berlin: Dietz Verlag), 23:165–66. *Capital*, in *Selected Writings*, ed. David McLellan (New York: Oxford University Press, 1977), 448. Translation lightly modified.

28. Gilles Deleuze and Félix Guattari, *Anti-Oedipus: Capitalism and Schizophrenia*, trans. Robert Hurley, Mark Seem, and Helen R. Lane (Minneapolis: University of Minnesota Press, 1983), 180 and 197.

29. Deleuze borrows the notion of the "mutual image" from Gaston Bachelard's *La Terre et les reveries de la volonté*. The expression appears four times in the chapter we are reading ("The Crystals of Time"), then twice in the "Conclusions" that close *Time-Image*. We should re-read here the pages from Émile Benveniste, in *Indo-European Language and Society*, trans. Elizabeth Palmer (London: Faber and Faber, 1973) on the Latin adjective *mutuus*, which "indicates either 'loan' or 'borrowing'" (149) just as it "qualifies what is to be replaced by an equivalent" (150).

30. Recall as well this other passage we have already read: "Thus the image has to be present and past, still present and already past, *at once and at the same time* [my emphasis]. If it was not already past at the same time as present, the present would never pass on. . . . The present is the actual image, and *its* contemporaneous past is the virtual image, the image in a mirror" (*Time-Image*, 79).

31. Deleuze, you will have noticed, regularly insists upon the close inter-belonging of the actual and the virtual, marks the mutuality of their exchange, by writing the possessive adjective or relative pronoun that connects them in italics: "The actual image and *its* virtual image" (*Time-Image*, 73); "The present is the actual image, and *its* contemporaneous past is the virtual image" (82); "In contrast, the virtual image in the pure state is defined . . . in accordance with the actual present *of which* it is the past" (83); "a small internal circuit between a present and *its own* past, between an actual image and *its* virtual image" (84); "the actual and *its* virtual on the small circuit" (84). But at least once he replaces the italics with quotation marks: "The crystal-image . . . consists in the indivisible unity of an actual image and 'its' virtual image" (82). These quotation marks seem, on the contrary, to indicate the distance from the virtual image, which precisely no longer belongs entirely to the actual, which separates from it, which is "its" only in a manner of speaking. This hesitation in the punctuation of exchange (which I will return to in the next lecture) reflects very precisely the tension at work in its punctiformity.

32. This is how I would be tempted to gloss these most difficult of sentences (we have already read some of them) in the middle of the fourth chapter of *Time-Image*: "If it is true that movement maintains a set of exchanges or an equivalence, a symmetry as an invariant, time is by nature the conspiracy

of unequal exchange or the impossibility of an equivalence. . . . *The cinema
confronts its most internal presupposition, money, and the movement-image makes
way for the time-image in one and the same operation.* What the film within the
film expresses is this infernal circuit between the image and money, this
inflation which time puts into the exchange. . . . The film is movement, but
the film within the film is money, is time" (81).

2. THE POINT OF (NO) EXCHANGE, OR THE DEBT-IMAGE

1. We could—still another experience of thinking—transpose the scene of
walking I am describing to elocution or conversation, in terms of an old analogy Balzac formulated in his "Theory of Walking," published in 1833: "Isn't
speech in a sense the gait of the heart and brain?" Cadence is where the foot
or voice falls (*cadere* in Latin), where they rest, settle. And cadence, as theo-
rists of music have emphasized at length, is a matter of punctuation. Thus,
Antoine Reicha has noted that "cadences, in Music, are closely analogous to
grammatical punctuation" (*Traité de mélodie, abstraction faite de ses rapports avec
l'harmonie* [Paris: Imprimerie de J. L. Scherff, 1814], 12). And he adds: "That
is why one could call a quarter cadence [that is, a barely marked rest on a
given note of the scale] a comma, and designate it with the sign (,); a half
cadence with the sign (;) or a colon (:), and the perfect cadence with the period
(.)." Cadence, walking, as well as everything I will analyze later as a *point of
(no) exchange*, fall under the "general stigmatology" that I sketched out in *Of
Stigmatology: Punctuation as Experience*, trans. Jan Plug (New York: Fordham
University Press, 2018), 100–101. There, I emphasized its *economic* import,
from the origins of punctuation in the practice of accounting to what Heidegger, in "European Nihilism," expressed in these terms: "There are view-
points only for a seeing that points [*für ein Sehen, daß punktiert*] and calculates
by means of points [*nach "Punkten" rechnen muß*]." See Heidegger, "European
Nihilism," in *Nietzsche*, vol. 3, ed. David Farrell Krell (New York: Harper
Collins, 1991).

2. My thanks to Laura Odello for drawing my attention to this remarkable
televisual moment.

3. G. W. F. Hegel, *Phenomenology of Spirit*, trans. A. V. Miller (New York:
Oxford University Press), 113–14.

4. Szendy quotes the French translation by Jean Hyppolite: *Phénoménologie
de l'esprit* (Paris: Aubier-Montaigne), 1:156.—Trans.

5. Hyppolite translates *Wechsel* as "change" and *Austauschung* as "permutation" (159). Bernard Bourgeois confuses these distinct terms by proposing
"exchange" for both—he thus makes them interchangeable, as it were (in *Phénoménologie de l'esprit*, trans. Bernard Bourgeois [Paris: Vrin, 2006], 202). As

for Jean-Pierre Lefebvre, for *Wechsel*, he sometimes chooses "alternation" and sometimes "change," but keeps "exchange" for *Austauschung* (*Phénoménologie de l'esprit*, trans. Jean-Pierre Lefebvre [Paris: Aubier, 1991], 133 and 151).

6. Susan Sontag, *On Photography* (New York: Farrar, Straus and Giroux, 1977), 15.

7. I will not necessarily follow Sontag in her diagnosis of what she calls our "sad, frightened time" (*On Photography*, 14), a diagnosis that leads to regrets of this sort: "Now nature—tamed, endangered, mortal—needs to be protected from people. When we are afraid, we shoot. But when we are nostalgic, we take pictures" (15). I recall, rather, that Jules-Étienne Marey in 1882 invented a "photographic gun." The cinema before cinema thus relied on a multiple shot, a *flurry*, whose memory survives, in the form of a mediologic unconscious, in so many scenes of photocinematographic shootings: I am thinking especially of the epilogue to the series *Breaking Bad*, which shows the pure movements of an automatic rifle that fires its bursts of flashes and those of a massage chair equipped with a sort of artificial respiration that seems to raise dead bodies.

8. On August 20, 1983, Leone published a tribute in *Corriere della sera* titled "To John Ford."

9. The French *règlement de comptes* is at once a settling of scores or, more literally, of accounts, and a gunfight.—Trans.

10. See "Exchange and Equity" (in "The Wanderer and His Shadow") in Nietzsche, *Human, All Too Human*, trans. Gary Handwerk (Stanford, Calif.: Stanford University Press, 2013), 2:168–69. About twenty years after Nietzsche, Marx in his *Grundrisse*, composed between October 1857 and May 1858, attempted to show how money unbalanced the supposed immediacy of exchange:

> Just as the exchange value of a commodity leads a double existence, as the particular commodity and as money, so does the act of exchange split [*so zerfällt der Akt des Austauschs*] into two mutually independent acts: exchange of commodities for money, exchange of money for commodities; purchase and sale. Since these have now acquired a spatially and temporally separate and mutually indifferent form of existence, their immediate identity [*unmittelbare Identität*] ceases. They may correspond or not; they may balance or not; they may enter into disproportion with one another [*in Mißverhältnisse zueinander treten*]. They will of course always attempt to equalize one another [*auszugleichen*], but in the place of earlier immediate equality [*an die Stelle der frühern unmittelbaren Gleichheit*] there now stands the constant movement of equalization [*die beständige Bewegung der Ausgleichung*], which evidently presupposes continual non-equivalence [*beständige Ungleichsetzung*]. It is now entirely possible that consonance [*Konsonanz*] may be reached only by passing through the most extreme

dissonance [*der äußersten Dissonanzen*]. (Karl Marx, *Grundrisse: Foundations of the Critique of Political Economy*, trans. Martin Nicolaus [New York: Random House, 1973], 148)

The apparently lost immediacy, however, actually seems to remain for Marx the ground of exchange, since it is only divided and carried over to the two moments of exchange in question (commodities for money and money for commodities), which in turn continue to assume that immediacy.

11. The sequence in which he learns to shoot, where Doniphon tries to teach Ransom to handle a revolver, convinces us of this. "Balance it in your hand," he advises his protégé. Shooting well is above all a matter of finding one's balance.

12. Hegel, *Phenomenology of Spirit*, 115.

13. But it is a debt whose possibility is nevertheless rooted in what we would have to call, with a certain Marx, the *fiction* of exchange. One could in fact cite countless passages in which Marx, especially in the *Grundrisse*, analyzes how capital "obtains . . . a value for which it has given no equivalent": "Surplus value [*Mehrwert*] in general is value [*Wert*] in excess of the equivalent [*über das Äquivalent hinaus*]. The equivalent, by definition, is only the identity of value with itself [*die Identität des Werts mit sich*]. Hence surplus value can never sprout out of the equivalent" (324). Surplus value is thus created from the difference between the minimum pay necessary to "keep alive [*am Leben zu erhalten*]" the worker—it might correspond to "half a day" of his work, for example—and the additional time he gives without exchange (that he is *forced* to give: It is a debt that never speaks its name):

> The capitalist has paid the price of only half a working day but has obtained a whole day objectified [*vergegenständlichte*] in the product; thus has exchanged *nothing* [nichts *ausgetauscht hat*] for the second half of the work day. The only thing which can make him into a capitalist is not exchange [*Austausch*], but rather a process through which he obtains *objectified labour time*, i.e. *value*, without exchange. (324)

However, exchange is a fiction necessary for the existence of capital: "On the other hand, *without* exchange the production of capital as such would not exist, since *realization* as such [*die* Verwertung *als solche*] cannot exist without exchange" (447). "This exchange of equivalents [*Austausch von Äquivalenten*] . . . is only the surface layer [*oberflächliche Schichte*] of a production which rests on the appropriation of alien labour *without exchange*, but with the *semblance of exchange* [*auf der Aneignung fremder Arbeit* ohne Austausch]" (509). Deleuze of course has Marx's formulations in view in the pages we have read from *Time-Image*. We still have to draw the conclusions for what I will call, with or beyond Benjamin, "cine-capital." "Das Filmkapital," he writes at the end of the fifth section of the first version of "The Work of Art in the Age of Its Technological Reproducibility." I will attempt to understand this word in the most rigorous iconomic manner, as does my friend Jun Fujita in his beautiful book *Cine-capital: Cómo las imágenes devienen revolucionarias* (Buenos Aires: Tinta Limón, 2014).

14. Rudolf Arnheim, "Ein Blick in die Ferne," in *Die Seele in der Silber-schicht: Medientheoretische Texte* (Frankfurt am Main: Suhrkamp, 2004), 354–69. The article appeared in *Intercine* 2 (February 1935): 71–82.

15. How can we not think, here, of Paul Valéry's words cited by Benjamin in the final versions of his essay "The Work of Art in the Age of Its Techno-logical Reproducibility": "Just as water, gas, and electricity are brought into our houses from far off to satisfy our needs with minimal effort, so we shall be supplied with visual or auditory images, which will appear and disappear at a simple movement of the hand, hardly more than a sign" (Walter Benjamin, *Selected Works*, ed. Howard Eiland and Michael W. Jennings [Cambridge, Mass.: Harvard University Press, 2003], 4:253). See Paul Valéry, "La conquête de l'ubiquité," in *Oeuvres* (Paris: Gallimard, 1960), 2:1284. This vertiginous circulation of the iconomic tide makes our gaze into the market of what we could call a mass iconomy.

3. INNERVATION, OR THE GAZE OF CAPITAL

1. Gilles Deleuze, "Letter to Serge Daney," in *Gilles Deleuze: Negotiations 1972–1990*, trans. Martin Joughin (New York: Columbia University Press, 1995), 75–76, translation modified). See also: "The world really is turning into film, is constantly moving in that direction, and that's just what television amounts to, the whole world turning into film" (78, translation modified). Deleuze's letter was intended as the preface for Daney's book *Ciné Journal: 1981–1986* (Paris: Cahiers du Cinéma, 1986).

2. The French *travelling* is a technical term from cinema for a dolly, travel-ing platform, or tracking shot.—Trans.

3. According to the online *Trésor de la langue française* (completed in 2002 and available at http://atilf.atilf.fr/tlf.htm), *innervation*, the word we will be considering at length, appeared for the first time in French in the fourth edi-tion of Pierre-Hubert Nyssen's *Dictionnaire de médecine, de chirurgie, de phar-macie, des sciences accessoires et de l'art vétérinaire* (Paris: J. A. Brosson and J.-S. Chaudé, 1824). There we find this definition: "INNERVATION, fem. noun *innervatio*, from *in*, in, and *nervus*, nerve. This word designates the nervous influx necessary to maintain life and the various organ functions." I have found at least one earlier occurrence of the word, however, in the grammarian

Pierre Morel's *Essai sur les voix de la langue française* (Paris: Le Normant, 1804), 17. I mention it for two reasons. On the one hand, like Benjamin in a passage we will be reading, the author establishes a parallel between innervation and electricity: "The word *innervation* . . . like the word *electricity* has the advantage of representing that part of matter that serves . . . as a conductor" (17). And on the other hand, Morel inscribes this notion in an economic perspective (in the sense in which, since the seventeenth century, the "animal economy" has designated the study of the bodies and movements of animals): "Is innervation . . . scattered diffusely throughout the entire economy, or is it contained within certain organs that create or at least distribute it?"

4. Walter Benjamin, "Fragmente vermischten Inhalts: Zur Ästhetik," *Gesammelte Schriften* (Frankfurt am Main: Suhrkamp, 1991), 6:126–27. In a remarkable archaeology of the concept of medium in Benjamin and beyond, Antonio Somaini offers a rigorous reading of this fragment. Somaini, "'L'oggetto attualmente più importante dell'estetica': Benjamin, il cinema come *Apparat* e il '*Medium* della percezione,'" *Fata morgana* 20 (2013): 117–46.

5. See, especially, the essay "Über Sprache überhaupt und über die Sprache des Menschen," in *Gesammelte Schriften*, 2:142. "On Language as Such and on the Language of Man," in *Selected Writings*, ed. Marcus Bullock and Michael W. Jennings (Cambridge, Mass.: Harvard University Press, 1996): "All language is in the purest sense the 'medium' of the communication [*das 'Medium' der Mitteilung*]. Mediation [*das Mediale*: the medial or mediumness as such], which is the *immediacy* of all mental communication [*ist die* Unmittelbarkeit *aller geistigen Mitteilung*], is the fundamental problem of linguistic theory" (1:64).

6. In his meditation on touching in Jean-Luc Nancy, Jacques Derrida thus speaks of "a disadhering [*désadhérance*], a *différance* in the very 'inside' of haptics—and *aisthēsis* in general": "Whatever concrete, 'technical,' or 'prosthetic' form it wears to determine itself between a skin and something, or between two skins (instruments, veils, clothing, gloves, condoms, and so on), this *différance* of the *between*, this elementary *différance* of inter-position or intervals between two surfaces is at the same time the condition of contact and the originally spaced opening that calls for technical prosthetics and makes it possible, without any delay." Derrida, *On Touching—Jean-Luc Nancy*, trans. Christine Irizarry (Stanford, Calif.: Stanford University Press, 2000), 229–30.

7. Walter Benjamin, *One-Way Street*, trans. Edmund Jephcott, ed. Michael W. Jennings (Cambridge, Mass.: Harvard University Press, 2016), 45. On the chronology of the occurrences of the word *Innervation* in Benjamin and its stakes, see the excellent analysis by Miriam Bratu Hansen, "Mistaking the Moon for a Ball," in *Cinema and Experience: Siegfried Kracauer,*

Walter Benjamin, and Theodor W. Adorno (Berkeley: University of California Press, 2011), 132–46. Hansen does not, however, mention Benjamin's review of Ramón Gómez de la Serna's book *Le Cirque*. In that account, which appeared in 1927 in *Internationale Revue*, published in Amsterdam, we read: "In the circus, even the most narrow minded has to understand to what extent certain physical performances are closer to what is essential—to wonder, so to speak—than phenomena of interiority, which are sometimes merely the banal form that such innervations assume in the eyes of the idealist [*Im Zirkus muß ja selbst dem Borniertesten aufgehen, um wie viel näher am Wesentlichen, wenn man will am Wunder, gewisse physische Leistungen stehen als die Phänomene der Innerlichkeit, die manchmal nur die banale Erscheinungsform sind, die solche Innervationen in den Augen des Idealisten besitzen*]." Benjamin, *Gesammelte Schriften*, 3:70. It is difficult to determine if this occurrence of the word precedes that in *One-Way Street*, which was published in 1928 but drafted earlier: A partial version of *One-Way Street*, which appeared under the title *Bemerkungen* in *Magdeburgische Zeitung*, November 10, 1927, contains the aphorisms grouped under the rubric *Antiquitäten*, where the word also appears: "No representation without innervation [*keine Vorstellung ohne Innervation*]." *Gesammelte Schriften*, 4:117.

8. Benjamin, *Gesammelte Schriften*, 6:188–90. "Notes on a Theory of Gambling," in *Selected Writings*, 2:297.

9. In an earlier note titled "<Tele>pathie," Benjamin already insisted, though without using the word *Innervation*, upon the necessity of thinking gambling as an unconscious process: "A game hall is an exceptional laboratory for telepathic experiments," he wrote, before adding that the good "attitude [*Haltung*]" toward gambling, the winning attitude, "cannot be conquered from inside by stubbornness [that is, through conscious will], to which the losing gambler frequently has recourse, thus only losing more." *Gesammelte Schriften*, 6:187–88. One will of course recall the importance Freud also placed upon telepathy. See my *Phantom Limbs: On Musical Bodies*, trans. Will Bishop (New York: Fordham University Press, 2015), where I ventured, in the chapter "Telepathy," a first and provisional reading of Benjamin's two fragments on innervation and gambling. I also brought in a later work that echoes these two fragments, "The Lucky Hand [Die glückliche Hand]," a story Benjamin probably intended for *Frankfurter Zeitung* in 1935. There, one can read: "If there really is such a thing as a lucky gambler, that is, a telepathic mechanism [*einen telepathischen Mechanismus*] in gambling, then it resides in the unconscious [*so sitzt der im Unbewußten*]. It is unconscious knowledge that, if played successfully, translates itself into movements [*sich in Bewegungen umsetzt*]. If on the other hand it migrates to the consciousness, then it is lost

for innervation [*setzt es sich dagegen in das Bewußtsein um, so geht es für die Innervation verloren*]. Our man will 'think' the correct thing but he will 'act' wrongly. He will stand there like so many other losers who tear their hair out and cry 'I knew it!'" *Gesammelte Schriften*, 4:775. *The Storyteller: Tales out of Loneliness*, ed. and trans. Sam Dolbear, Esther Leslie, and Sebastian Truskolaski (New York: Verso, 2016).

10. Benjamin, *Gesammelte Schriften*, 6:189. *Selected Writings*, 2:298.

11. In a beautiful book (*Body- and Image-Space: Re-reading Walter Benjamin* [New York: Routledge, 1996]), Sigrid Weigel shows very convincingly how Benjamin, without always referring explicitly to Freud (and even "less so where traces of the figures of Freudian thinking are more influential in his work"), borrows numerous Freudian concepts, notably those that are important for us here, that is, "facilitation" [*Bahnung*, i.e., "pathbreaking"] and "innervation" (106–7). Yet the word *facilitation* occurs very rarely in Benjamin's work. Weigel quotes only one occurrence (112), from *Berliner Chronik* [*Berlin Chronicle*]: the verb *bahnen* (*Gesammelte Schriften*, 6:491). The most important occurrence, for our purposes here (Weigel doesn't mention it), is found in an unpublished manuscript variant of "Painting and Photography" (*Gesammelte Schriften*, 7:818). Quoting Henry Wallon's reflections (in "Psychologie et technique," in *À la lumière du marxisme* [Paris: Editions Sociales Internationales, 1935], 145, 147) on the metamorphosis of visual perception brought on by the experience of aviation (see also *Gesammelte Schriften*, 3:583, where we find the same citation), Benjamin notes that these metamorphoses "also hold for someone who has never sat in an airplane [*auch für den gelten, der niemals in einem Flugzeug gesessen hat*], for nothing stops this person from opening a path [*den Weg zu bahnen*] through empathy [*Einfühlung*] for the new automatisms of our perceptive mechanism's reactions." A few lines later, however, film is charged with transmitting new sensory experiences to vision: "Even the most moving and dramatic views of the airfield are already given by the camera, which then communicates them to the human eye [*gerade die bewegtesten und spannungsreichsten Ansichten des Fluggeländes bieten sich sonach zuerst der Kamera, die sie dann dem menschlichen Auge mitteilt*]."

12. Sigmund Freud, *Studies on Hysteria*, in *The Standard Edition of the Complete Psychological Works of Sigmund Freud*, ed. James Strachey (London: Hogarth, 1955), 2:285.

13. It figures in the "Catalogue of Works Read" that Benjamin himself compiled. See "Verzeichnis der gelesenen Schriften," in *Gesammelte Schriften*, 7:440, 443. See Sigmund Freud, *Jokes and Their Relation to the Unconscious*, in *The Standard Edition of the Complete Psychological Works of Sigmund Freud*, ed. James Strachey (London: Hogarth, 1955), 8:79–80.

14. Sigmund Freud, *The Neuro-Psychoses of Defense*, in *The Standard Edition of the Complete Psychological Works of Sigmund Freud*, ed. James Strachey, vol. 3 (London: Hogarth, 1955). Freud speaks of electricity as having "utility in . . . explaining [*Hilfsvorstellung*]," the neuroses of defense (3:61). In the "mental functions," he says, "something is to be distinguished . . . which is capable of increase, diminution, displacement, and discharge, and which is spread over the memory-traces of ideas somewhat as an electrical charge [*wie eine eleck-trische Ladung*] is spread over the surface of a body" (3:60). This hypothesis, he adds, can be "used in the same way that physicists apply the hypothesis of a flow of electrical fluid [*des strömenden elektrischen Fluidums*]" (3:61).

15. "In the age of Napoleon, electricity had roughly the same significance as Christianity in the age of Tiberius. Gradually it became apparent that this general innervation of the world was of greater consequence and better able to change the future than any 'political' event from Ampère to the present day." Paul Valéry, "Regards sur le monde actuel," in *Oeuvres* (Paris: Gallimard, 1960), 2:919–20. Quoted in Benjamin, "Paul Valéry. Zu seinem 60. Geburtstag," *Gesammelte Schriften*, 2:390. *Selected Writings*, 2:534. Translation lightly modified.

16. See "A Case of Successful Treatment by Hypnotism," in *The Standard Edition of the Complete Psychological Works of Sigmund Freud*, ed. James Strachey, vol. 1 (London: Hogarth, 1966) and *Studies on Hysteria*. If I linger over Freud's early works, which Benjamin does not mention in his "Catalogue of Works Read," it is because, as Weigel emphasizes, the "neurological variant of psychoanalysis, in which bodily processes were attributed greater significance, evidently played a role in Benjamin's earliest studies of Freud during his university years in Bern, as the notes on anthropology composed at this time demonstrate" (*Body- and Image-Space*, 122). In *Acta muriensa*, a satire he wrote with his friend Gershom Scholem between 1918 and 1923, we find the teaching program for the imaginary university of Muri (a small city close to Bern), including seminars by "Professor Sigmund Freud" titled "Where Small Children Come From [*Woher kommen die kleinen Kinder*]" and "Explanations of Selected Jokes." Benjamin, *Gesammelte Schriften*, 4:442. I take the expression *agent voyer* from Gilles Deleuze and Félix Guattari (it is how they describe the State in *A Thousand Plateaus*). A strange and anachronistic meeting between Deleuze and Benjamin (by way of Bergson, through Bergsonian pathways) lies ahead of us. It will be evoked later. Or better, it will impose itself. [The published translation of *A Thousand Plateaus* translates *agent voyer* as "town surveyor." See *A Thousand Plateaus: Capitalism and Schizophrenia*, trans. Brian Massumi (Minneapolis: University of Minnesota Press, 1987). —Trans.].

17. Benjamin, *Gesammelte Schriften*, 2:766. *Selected Writings*, 2:204.

18. Benjamin, *Gesammelte Schriften*, 2:763; *Selected Writings*, 2:201.

19. Breuer, in one of the sections of *Studies on Hysteria* he was responsible for ("Theoretical Observations"), several times has recourse to the metaphor of the short circuit to explain certain hysterical phenomena. See *Studies on Hysteria* in *The Standard Edition of the Complete Psychological Works of Freud*, vol. 2, ed. James Strachey (London: Hogarth, 1955).

20. Benjamin, "Der Sürrealismus. Die letzte Momentaufnahme der europäischen Intelligenz," in *Gesammelte Schriften*, 2:308–10. "Surrealism: The Last Snapshot of the European Intelligentsia," in *Selected Writings of Walter Benjamin*, 2:207–21, translation modified.

21. See Rainer Nägele, "Body Politics: Benjamin's Dialectical Materialism between Brecht and the Frankfurt School," in *The Cambridge Companion to Walter Benjamin*, ed. David Ferris (Cambridge: Cambridge University Press, 2006): "If the space of political action is a 'hundred percent image space,' there is no room left for a political 'reality,' on the one hand, and its representation in images, metaphors, and similes, on the other. . . . This image space is structured like a language of the unconscious, marked by jokes and 'Freudian' slips. . . . The image is thus not the representation of something, but its exposition in the act itself. It is a particular kind of act: the image of true presentation appears not in the intentional act but, as in psychoanalysis, in a slip, in an *acte manqué*" (172).

22. To my knowledge, Deleuze mentions Benjamin but once in the entirety of his two volumes on cinema, and there it is essentially to say that Syberberg "goes farther" than Benjamin, "launching the theme 'Hitler as filmmaker'" (*Time-Image*, 264, 330n5). Benjamin is barely more present in *The Fold: Leibniz and the Baroque* (trans. Tom Conley [Minneapolis: University of Minnesota Press, 1988], 125), when Deleuze speaks of baroque allegory. See also the passage from *Time-Image* on "industrial art" and "the internalized relation with money" (we read this during the first lecture), where Benjamin is clearly the target although he is not named explicitly (*Time-Image*, 77).

23. We know that Deleuze's meditation on cinema takes place under the aegis of Bergson. Less explicitly but just as decisively, Benjamin's article on surrealism is full of Bergsonism, as witnessed by a notebook in which Benjamin emphasizes "Bergson's influence on surrealism" (*Gesammelte Schriften*, 2:1022). Later, in the 1940 "On Some Motifs in Baudelaire" (1:608–9), Benjamin devotes a few important pages to *Matter and Memory*, which is also mentioned in the *Arcades Project* (5:272, 1008). To be sure, the concept of *Bildraum* also has its own history in Benjamin. Thus, we find three—cursory and rather indeterminate—occurrences of the word in a posthumous fragment on painting ("Zur Malerei," 6:114), which the editors of the *Gesammelte Schriften* date to 1919–21. And it could also be shown that, even if it isn't mentioned by

name, the concept is prefigured in the fragments on blushing ("Über die Scham," 6:70, and "Erröten in Zorn und Scham," 6:120). For what is it to blush if not to produce an image that would be translated *immediately* on the surface of the body? It is in this sense, moreover, and according to the paradoxical logic of immediation we are now familiar with, that blushing for Benjamin is also a matter of "medium [*Medium*]." See "Über die Malerei oder Zeichen und Mal," 2:605. However, as James McFarland notes very accurately, when, at the end of his essay on surrealism, "Benjamin invokes the 'image space,' . . . he is using Bergson's concepts." See McFarland, *Critical Theory to Structuralism*, ed. David Ingram (New York: Routledge, 2014), 123. We should take the time to compare Deleuze's Bergsonian idea that "my eye, my brain are images"—and are therefore *in* the image—with the Benjaminian motif that appears with the 1915 fictive dialogue between Margarethe and Georg, in "The Rainbow," that is, that the viewer is dissolved in viewing (7:20): "So it was in my dream. I was nothing but seeing [*Ich war nichts als Sehen*]. I was not a viewer, I was only viewing [*Ich war keine Sehende, ich war nur Sehen*]. And what I saw were not things, Georg, only colors. And I myself was colored in this landscape" (Benjamin, "The Rainbow: Dialogue on Fantasy," trans. Peter Fenves, in Fenves, *The Messianic Reduction: Walter Benjamin and the Shape of Time* [Stanford, Calif.: Stanford University Press, 2011], 247–48). I will limit myself here to recalling two passages from Deleuze's *Cinema 1: The Movement-Image*, trans. Hugh Tomlinson and Barbara Habberjam (Minneapolis: University of Minnesota, 1986) that say nothing else. First this one: "How could my brain contain images, since it is one image among others? . . . how could images be in my consciousness, since I am myself image, that is, movement" (58). And then this: "They are images in themselves. If they do not appear to anyone, that is, to an eye, this is because . . . the eye is in things, in luminous images themselves" (60).

24. Karl Marx and Friedrich Engels, *Ökonomisch-philosophische Manuskripte aus dem Jahre 1844*, in *Werke*, 40:540. *Collected Works*, 3:302.

25. It is indeed a question of how perception *is organized* (soon, in fact, we will speak of an *organology of the sensible*) and not of how it "operates" (as in Rainer Rochlitz's French translation [the one used by Szendy—trans.]).

26. In "On the Doctrine of Revolutions as Innervations of the Collective" (in *The Arcades Project*, trans. Howard Eiland and Kevin McLaughlin [Cambridge, Mass.: Harvard University Press, 1999], X 1a, 2, 652), Benjamin quotes Marx's *1844 Manuscript*, which was published in two volumes in Leipzig in 1932: Karl Marx, *Der historische Materialismus: Die Frühschriften*. We find there, interspersed with ellipses where Benjamin omits phrases, well-known formulations: "*Außer diesen unmittelbaren Organen bilden sich daher gesellschaftliche Organe. . . . Es versteht sich, daß das menschliche Auge anders gefaßt, als das*

rohe, unmenschliche Auge, das menschliche Ohr anders als das rohe Ohr, etc.
[Besides these direct organs, therefore, *social* organs develop. . . . It is obvious
that the *human* eye enjoys things in a way different from that of the crude,
nonhuman eye; the human *ear* different from the crude ear; and so on]."
Probably between 1935 and 1937, Benjamin recopied this quote (interestingly,
the dating by the editors of the *Gesammelte Schriften* [vol. 5, 1262] is based on
changes in photographic technology, for Benjamin had his manuscript photographed in order to save it, as we would do today with a USB stick or an external hard drive). The quote thus dates to the same years as the first version of
the artwork essay. Another occurrence of the word *innervation* is found in
W 7, 4, in the convolute *Fourier.* There too, Benjamin speaks "of revolution as
an innervation of the technical organs of the collective [*von der Revolution als
einer Innervation der technischen Organe des Kollektivs*]" (631).

27. See Peter Szendy, *Phantom Limbs: On Musical Bodies*, trans. Will Bishop
(New York: Fordham University Press, 2015), where I suggested that the concept of "organology" be broadened in the direction of a "general organology
of the senses" (133), which Bernard Stiegler took up in *De la misère symbolique*,
volumes 1 and 2 (Paris: Galilée, 2004 and 2005).

28. Benjamin, "Das Kunstwerk im Zeitalter seiner Technischen Reproduzierbarkeit," in *Gesammelte Schriften*, 1:444–45.

29. Benjamin, "L'Oeuvre d'art à l'époque de sa reproduction mécanisée,"
in *Gesammelte Schriften*, trans. Pierre Klossowski (1936), 1:717.

30. Thus, one reads in the French version: "The painter is to the operator
what the mage is to the surgeon. The former preserves in his work a normal
distance with regard to the reality of his subject—however, the cameraman
penetrates profoundly into the tissue of given reality" (1:728).

31. Benjamin, *Gesammelte Schriften*, 1:480. *Selected Writings*, 4:256.

32. See Benjamin, *Gesammelte Schriften*, vol. 1:443. *Selected Writings*, 3:106.

33. See Benjamin, *Gesammelte Schriften*, 1:443: "Art history might be seen
as the working out of a tension between two polarities within the artwork
itself, its course being determined by shifts between the two. These two poles
are the artwork's cult value and its exhibition value. Artistic production
begins with figures in the service of magic. *What is important for these figures is
that they are present, not that they are seen* [my emphasis]. . . . Certain statues of
gods are accessible only to the priest in the cella; certain images of the
Madonna remain covered nearly all year round; certain sculptures on medi-
eval cathedrals are not visible to the viewer at ground level." *Selected Writings*,
3:106. Emphasis added. [Here the translation of the second version of the
essay is quoted, as it corresponds closely to the first version cited by the
author.—Trans.]

34. Benjamin, *Gesammelte Schriften*, 1:444.

35. In this sense, the other iconomic limit, that of pure exhibition value, would also amount to removing the image from its visibility, but for reasons that are opposed or symmetrical to those that govern its pure use value in the cult: It becomes anoptic not by withdrawing into the invisibility of the sacred, but because its overexhibition causes it to lapse into the distraction of the tactile, causes it to *change sense* [meaning, direction, sense], transfers it into another region of *aisthēsis* (while at the same time upending the general organization of the sensible).

36. The word *innervation* is no longer found in the fourth and final version of the artwork essay from 1938. And it makes its final appearance with a single occurrence in "On Some Motifs in Baudelaire" ("Über einige Motive bei Baudelaire," 1:630), when Benjamin calls to mind the "innervations that flow through him [the pedestrian in the big city] in rapid succession [*durchzucken ihn . . . Innervationen in rascher Folge*]." The following phrase immediately recalls Baudelaire's image of the man who dives into the crowd "as into a reservoir of electric energy [*wie in ein Reservoir elektrischer Energie*]." *Selected Writings*, 4:328. Translation modified.

37. The expression *Medium des Marktes* appears only once, to my knowledge, in one of the fragments of *Central Park* [*Zentralpark*] (April 1938–39). *Zentralpark*, in *Gesammelte Schriften*, 1:665. "Central Park," in *Selected Writings*, 4:168. As for Marx, in the second volume of *Capital*, at the end of chapter 18, he speaks of the "medium of money [*Geldmedium*]." See *Das Kapital*, vol. 2 in Marx and Engels, *Werke*, 24:358. Marx also describes money as the "circulating medium [*zirkulierendes Medium*]" (24:418).

38. In their *The Language of Psychoanalysis* (trans. Donald Nicholson-Smith [New York: W. W. Norton, 1973)], Jean Laplanche and Jean-Bertrand Pontalis emphasize that the term *conversion*—which in hysteria designates "a transposition of a psychical conflict into, and its attempted resolution through, somatic symptoms"—for Freud is "tied to an *economic* approach: the libido detached from the repressed idea is transformed into an innervational energy" (90).

39. Benjamin, *Gesammelte Schriften*, 1:440.

40. In addition to the most literal sense of that which ensures exchange, the French *échangeur* also means *junction* or *intersection*.—Trans. See Deleuze, *Movement-Image*, 4, 22; and Deleuze, *Cinema 2: The Time-Image*, trans. Hugh Tomlinson and Robert Galeta (Minneapolis: University of Minnesota Press, 1989), 78. Marx speaks of money as a "general equivalent" (or a "universal equivalent," depending on the version), especially in the first book of *Capital*: "Playing the role of universal equivalent within the world of commodities becomes the specifically social role [of money]," he writes (*Werke*, 23:83).

41. Deleuze quotes the historian of cinema Lotte Eisner: "L'école expressioniste," in *Cinéma* 55, no. 1 (1955): 22. Eisner includes a priceless account of

the filming of *The Last Laugh* in her monograph on Murnau, *F. W. Murnau* (Ivry-sur-Seine: Le Terrain Vague, 1964). Robert Herlth, who worked as set designer with Murnau and his director of photography, Karl Freund, tell how they removed the camera from its solid base and from any fixed connection. He recalls in particular the filming of the opening sequence, which takes the spectator's point of view from the elevator going down in the foyer to the revolving door of the grand Atlantic Hotel, in Berlin: "'*Now* we know why you made an open elevator,' Murnau told me, smiling. The camera was placed on a bicycle and, pointed at the hotel lobby, goes down; it crosses the foyer to the doorman." *The Last Laugh* is one of the first films in which the camera is freed from its tethers in this way, giving it unheard of latitude in movement. In fact, it was literally called, in German, an "unchained camera [*entfesselte Kamera*]."

42. Benjamin, *Gesammelte Schriften*, 2:301. "Surrealism," in *Selected Writings*, 2:211.

43. Recall the famous prosopopoeia with which Dziga Vertov sang the glory of the ocular movement film made infinite. See Vertov, "The Council of Three," in *Kino-Eye: The Writings of Dziga Vertov*, ed. Annette Michelson, trans. Kevin O'Brien (Berkeley: University of California Press, 1984):

> I am kino-eye, I am a mechanical eye. I, a machine, show you the world as only I can see it.

> Now and forever, I free myself from human immobility, I am in constant motion, I draw near, then fall away from objects, I crawl under, I climb into them. I move apace with the muzzle of a galloping horse, I plunge full speed into a crowd, I outstrip running soldiers, I fall on my back, I ascend with an airplane, I plunge and soar together with plunging and soaring bodies. (17)

44. On the history of these mobilizations of the gaze, see Anne Friedberg's remarkable book *Window Shopping: Cinema and the Postmodern* (Berkeley: University of California Press, 1993), whose point of departure is "a fascination with the shared logic of moviegoing and the shopping mall" (xi). Indeed, Friedberg writes, "The multiplex cinema and the shopping mall . . . sell the pleasures of imaginary mobility" (xi). And she adds, "The *mobilized gaze* has a history, which begins well before the cinema and is rooted in other cultural activities that involve walking and travel" (2). Friedberg devotes a few wonderful pages to George Pal's film *The Time Machine* (*La machine à explorer le temps* [1960], based on Welles's novel), where she shows how the spatial mobilization of the gaze is transposed into mobility in time: "The first countershot, demonstrating the machine's effect, shows a blur in focus. The subjective experience of time travel is clearly equated with a camera effect" (104). And the chronological measurement of the hero's (George's) time travel is marked by the shop's window frame: "The shop window is the marker of temporality: the new, the already-past, the ever-same. The mannequin and the

shop window remain constant, the clothes and the accessories are the new and the already past" (106).

45. See Alfred Franklin, *Dictionnaire historique des arts, métiers, et professions exercés dans Paris depuis le treizième siècle* (Paris: H. Welter, 1905): "Elevators (manufacturers of): Elevators seem to date to the 17th century. A famous *Mazarinade* [*Mazarinades* were pamphlets criticizing Jules Mazarin—Trans.; a note tells us the Marzarinade in question is *Inventaire des merveilles du monde rencontrées dans le palais du cardinal Mazarin* (Paris: Rolin de la Haye, 1649)] cites, among the curiosities in the Mazarin palace, 'a chair that, if someone sat in it, went up or down thanks to hidden works that pull a rope, the floor having been cut away to allow this.' It wasn't long before others copied Mazarin, although the construction of these mechanisms left much to be desired. They were perfected above all by the ingenious Villayer, an academician more interested in mechanics than letters. Saint-Simon [in his *Notes sur le journal de Dangeau*, 3:295] erroneously credits him with 'inventing flying chairs that thanks to counterweights went up and down by themselves between two walls, to the floor one wishes, simply by one's weight when one sits in them, and stopped where one wished.' Elevators of this kind already existed in Paris, Versailles, and Chantilly" (46).

46. See Gustave Servois's biographical note in *Oeuvres de La Bruyère* (Paris: Hachette, 1865), 1:cvii: "In writing the portrait of *Hermippus*, la Bruyère allowed himself the malicious pleasure of giving a satirical portrait of . . . Villayer."

47. Rem Koolhaas, in *Delirious New York: A Retroactive Manifesto for Manhattan* (New York: Oxford University Press, 1978), nicely describes the theatrical character of the demonstration:

> Elisha Otis, the inventor, mounts a platform that ascends—the major part, it seems, of the demonstration. But when it has reached its highest level, an assistant presents Otis with a dagger on a velvet cushion.
>
> The inventor takes the knife, seemingly to attack the crucial element of his own invention: the cable that has hoisted the platform upward and that now prevents its fall. Otis cuts the cable; it snaps.
>
> Nothing happens, either to platform or to inventor.
>
> Invisible safety catches—the essence of Otis' brilliance—prevent the platform from rejoining the surface of the earth.
>
> Thus Otis introduces an invention in urban theatricality: the anti-climax as denouement, the non-event as triumph. (19)

48. Emile Zola, *Au Bonheur des dames (The Ladies' Delight)*, trans. Robin Buss (London: Penguin Classics, 2001), 231, 242.

49. Patent number 25 076, August 9, 1859, filed by Nathan Ames.

50. Patent number 470 918, March 15, 1892, filed by Jesse W. Reno.

51. This statement by the head of Field's maintenance division is quoted in William Leach, *Land of Desire: Merchants, Power, and the Rise of a New American Culture* (New York: Vintage, 1993), 74. The "elevator," as Rem Koolhaas will quite rightly say, "differentiates between levels" and allows "surfaces to multiply," to be "linked and connected almost imperceptibly." In François Chaslin, *Deux conversations avec Rem Koolhaas et caetera* (Paris: Sens & Tonka, 2001), 129. I want to thank my friend François Quintin for having drawn my attention to Koolhaas's remarkable analyses of the elevator (we will return to them).

52. Seeberger had bought the patent for a mechanical escalator taken out by George A. Wheeler in 1892. See *Up, Down, Across: Elevators, Escalators, and Moving Sidewalks*, ed. Alisa Goetz (London: Merrell, 2003): "In 1898, before working with Otis on the Paris escalator design, Seeberger had taken over inventor George Wheeler's patents for a step-type escalator. . . . The word 'Escalator' itself, so boldly planted over the Seeberger escalator in Paris, had been coined by Seeberger, who registered it with a capital 'E' as a trademarked name. Otis bought out Seeberger in 1910, and the company held the Escalator trademark until 1950 when a court ruled that the word had become generic and was in the public domain" (143).

53. See Leach, *Land of Desire*, 271–72. On the first escalator installed in Harrods, see Alexandra Artley (*The Golden Age of Shop Design: European Shop Interiors, 1880–1939* [New York: Whitney Library of Design, 1976]), who recounts this detail to recall the now forgotten impact of an invention that must have been destabilizing, to say the least: "After the installation of their first escalator in November 1898, two attendants were stationed at the top of it to revive alarmed customers with cognac and sel volatile" (8).

54. The director mentions this sequence of shots notably in an interview with Quentin Tarantino ("Emotion Pictures: Quentin Tarantino Talks to Brian De Palma," in Brian De Palma, *Interviews*, ed. Lawrence F. Knapp [Jackson: University Press of Mississippi, 2003]): "Al Pacino," he says, "had never done a complicated Steadicam shot like that in his life" (147).

55. "It is always a great moment in cinema," Deleuze writes, "when the camera leaves a character, and even turns its back on him, following its own movement at the end of which it will rediscover him" (*Movement-Image*, 23). This starts to get at what Deleuze calls "the essence of the cinematographic movement-image," that is, "extracting from vehicles or moving bodies the movement which is their common substance" (23). It is in precisely this sense that the camera is "a *general equivalent* of all the means of locomotion that it shows or that it makes use of" (22).

56. Built by the architect John C. Portman Jr., the Bonaventure Hotel opened in 1976. See Fredric Jameson, "Postmodernism, or The Cultural Logic of Late Capitalism," *New Left Review* 146 (July–August 1984).

57. Ibid., 83.

58. The revolving door was patented by Theophilus Van Kannel, who, in his patent of August 7, 1888 (number 387, 571), boasts as follows of the advantages of his invention: "The entrance to the structure, either from the inside or the outside [this expression tells us a great deal about the idea behind these revolving doors that, in trying to make passage more fluid, erase the distinction between inside and outside] is always free and unobstructed."

59. Rem Koolhaas and the Harvard Project on the City, *Mutations* (Barcelona and Bordeaux: Actar, 2000), 136. A number of texts gathered in *Mutations* are reprinted in the monumental *Harvard Design School Guide to Shopping* (Cologne: Taschen, 2001). Koolhaas, who sees in shopping "the last remaining form of public activity" (125), sometimes seems to want to return to the department store as a form of resistance to the mall, to the commercial center that is still more successful in fulfilling the equalizing and indifferentiating essence of the escalator. See Nathaniel Herzberg, "Rem Koolhaas, as du shopping," *Le Monde*, October 11, 2012: "For [Koolhaas], it is essential that the department store be defended against the shopping mall. The former is 'the final urban element in the historical chain of shopping; then the mall is tasked with de-urbanizing everything.' He explains: 'In its essence, the mall groups foreseeable activities. A repetitive, reproducible formula. The city, on the contrary, is unpredictable, random, characteristics, moreover, that are in the process of disappearing from current cities. That is why the future of the department store interests me a great deal.'"

60. See François Chaslin, *Deux conversations avec Rem Koolhaas*, 128. And Robert M. Vogel, "Up, Down, Across: Elevators, Escalators, and Moving Sidewalks at the National Building Museum, Washington, D.C.," *Technology and Culture* 45, no. 1 (2004): 154. The first movable sidewalk was installed by the architect Joseph Lyman Silsbee and the engineer Max Schmidt for the World's Fair in Chicago in 1893 and then rebuilt for the World's Fair in Paris in 1900, where it was photographed by Émile Zola. The negative taken by Zola is reproduced by Anne Friedberg in *Window Shopping*, where it is accompanied by the following caption: "The moving sidewalk transported spectators through the exhibition grounds as if they were goods on a conveyor belt" (85).

61. The first glass elevator on the exterior of a building seems to have been installed in 1956 on the façade of the El Cortez Hotel in San Diego. Three years after this panoramic elevator, the hotel owner, Harry Handlery, also had a travelator built that connected the building to the motel in front of it. Thus, the moving sidewalk and its vertical equivalent coexisted on the same site until the sidewalk was demolished in 1986, followed in 2000 by the removal of the elevator, to allow for the hotel to be restored to its original structure.

62. See Rem Koolhaas and Hal Foster, *Junkspace* with *Running Room* (London: Notting Hill Editions, 2013): "Continuity is the essence of junkspace; it exploits any invention that enables expansion, deploys the infrastructure of seamlessness: escalator, air conditioning . . ." (4).

63. See, for example, *Windows XP for Dummies*, 2nd ed. (Hoboken, N.J.: Wiley, 2004): "The scrollbar, which resembles a cutaway of an elevator shaft . . . , rests along the edge of all overstuffed windows. Inside the shaft, a little elevator (technically the *scroll box*) rides up and down as you page through your work." On eye tracking and its many commercial applications, see especially Andrew Duchowski, *Eye Tracking Methodology: Theory and Practice* (New York: Springer, 2002), especially 261ff. (*Marketing/Advertising*). Or, in the vein of "advice to e-retailers" one might, for example, have a glance, as it were, at the manual by François Scheid, Renaud Vaillant, and Grégoire de Montaigu, *Le Marketing digital* (Paris: Eyrolles, 2012): "In the first instance, the e-marketer can better understand the movements [of internet users, that is, potential clients] almost scientifically, with heatmapping. A heatmap is a representation of where and how long the gaze rests on a webpage or email. Heatmaps derive from eye tracking. . . . The study of eye tracking is made possible by an eye camera. . . . The goal is generally to highlight the trajectory the gaze takes" (243).

64. It's worth lingering a bit over the eye tracking sequence in Farocki's documentary. There, we see an eye on the screen, the same one as at the beginning of the film, with a sort of reticle that is reflected in the center of the iris. The voice-over speaks to the subject whose eye this is, the subject of the experiment, the person whose gaze is to be measured. It says, "Okay, look at the center dot; the upper left dot; the upper right dot; lower left dot; lower right dot." The eye blinks, the eyelid closes and reopens. The visual field is thus defined in its extreme limits and the mechanism that measures the gaze—the device that tracks the eye movements—is configured, as it were, ready to follow the movements of vision. Next shot: As we are shown three screens (on the right: the shopping mall; on the top left: the eye gazing; on the bottom left: the reticle that shows where the gaze falls on the picture of the mall), the voice-over explains: "They see a series of scenes . . . in a mall." The commercial scene and the filmic scene share the same vocabulary; the one expresses itself in terms of the other. A close-up of the subject gazing, whose eyes are moving in saccades. The voice continues: "They walk themselves from one scene to the next at their own pace, spending as much or as little time with each scene, and looking at it as they choose." Reverse angle shot on the screen showing the image of the mall as it is seen, with the reticle that is searching, that seems to be groping across the so-called "scene." *Cut.* We move to a sort of symmetrical sequence, just as fascinating, in which we participate in a kind of class, a lesson in how to organize a sales space

according to the points on which the client's eyes will stop. The apparent expert in the matter explains to a group of salespeople "how to emphasize certain neutral points in a room . . . or to make them disappear." And she quotes what she presents as a dictum, a law that is to be followed: "The feet only go where the eyes have already been [*die Füsse gehen nur dorthin, wo die Augen schon waren*]." My thanks to Christa Blümlinger for having allowed me to see Farocki's film; she shows how it stages a "semiology of disposition" ("Harun Farocki: Stratégies critiques," *Parachute* 111 (2003).

65. "To look is to labor," Jonathan Beller asserts in his wonderful book *The Cinematic Mode of Production: Attention Economy and the Society of the Spectacle* (Hanover, N.H.: Dartmouth College Press, 2012), 2. He suggests—although without making the effort to trace its material history—that this is a recent evolution: "The industrialization of vision has shifted gears," he writes, adding that "perception is increasingly bound to production" (3). Later, Beller cites Horkheimer and Adorno's famous sentence, according to which "Entertainment [*Amusement*] is the prolongation [*Verlängerung*] of work under late capitalism [*unterm Spätkapitalismus*]" (*Dialectic of Enlightenment: Philosophical Fragment*, trans. Edmund Jephcott [Stanford, Calif.: Stanford University Press, 2002], 109). Cinema, television, and the internet thus figure among the numerous technologies that capture and capitalize on attention: "Television, as a sort of second job, creates surplus value for capital that allows it to combat the falling rate of profit. . . . No wonder we spend too much time in . . . doing things like email, web-research, and the like. The increasing efficiency and development of new attention-siphoning technologies . . . literally represent an evolution in the form of capital" (206). I find it difficult to follow Beller, however, when he postulates a sort of Edenic or supralapsarian origin of the gaze that capitalism is supposed to have corrupted gradually: "The transformation of the visual from a zone of unalienated creative practice to one of alienated labor is the result of capital accumulation" (7). For a critical perspective on the growing field of study in "the economy of attention," see also Yves Citton's wonderful book, *Pour une écologie de l'attention* (Paris: Le Seuil, 2014) (Citton draws in particular on Beller's work).

MERCHANDISE: GODZILLA'S EYE

1. Quoted in Tom Shone, *Blockbuster: How the Jaws and Jedi Generation Turned Hollywood into a Boom-Town* (New York: Scribner, 2005), 267.

2. See Tim Carvell, "How Sony Created a Monster," *Fortune*, June 8, 1998, 162–70.

3. See Shone, *Blockbuster*, 270–72. Emmerich, interviewed by the author, declares, "Sony wanted to have a hit, but the audience feels it if the studio is trying too hard. They did that campaign because they had to sell merchandizing

products. It was like a movie and a product, which wasn't right. It didn't work" (270–71).

DELETED SCENES: DOORS AND SLIDE CHANGERS IN *PICKPOCKET* AND *OBSESSION*

1. Robert Bresson, "A Confrontation between Death and Life," in *Bresson on Bresson: Interviews, 1943–1983* (New York: New York Review of Books, 2016), 208.

2. "The organization of movement is the organization of its elements, or its intervals, into phrases. . . . A work is made of phrases, just as a phrase is made of intervals of movement" (Dziga Vertov, *Kino-Eye: The Writings of Dziga Vertov*, ed. Annette Michelsen, trans. Kevin O'Brien [Berkeley: University of California Press, 1984], 9). And again: "The eye submits to the will of the camera and is directed by it to those successive points of the action that, most succinctly and vividly, bring the film phrase to the height or depth of resolution" (16). In this unique shot in *Pickpocket*, the betweenness of the suspended syntax in a sense becomes the interval through which Jeanne leaves, an interval emphasized and ornamented by the pirouette she makes her little sister—who is not supposed to leave the apartment she was planning to flee—complete.

DELETED SCENES: THREE VARIATIONS ON TIME AND MONEY (ANTONIONI, DE PALMA, BRESSON)

1. I thank my friend Eyal Peretz, a great connoisseur of De Palma (see his *Becoming Visionary: Brian De Palma's Cinematic Education of the Senses* [Stanford, Calif.: Stanford University Press, 2008]), for reminding me of this.

2. The two other characters also in the scene, Tony's bodyguard and Seidelbaum's enforcer, Luis, moreover, discuss the film shoots Luis claims to have been in: "Back then I worked in pictures, down in Colombia. I was in that movie *Burn!* You ever see it? You saw me, with Marlon Brando? You know, we're good friends. I was his driver." The film in question, *Burn!*, was directed by Gillo Pontecorvo in 1969.

PHOTO GALLERY: *BLOW-UP*, OR WHY THERE ARE NO IMAGES

1. Roland Barthes, *Camera Lucida: Reflections on Photography*, trans. Richard Howard (New York: Hill and Wang, a division of Farrar, Straus and Giroux, 1981), 89. See also: "One day I received from a photographer a picture of myself which I could not remember being taken, for all my efforts. . . . And yet, *because it was a photograph* I could not deny that I had been *there* (even if I did not know *where*). This distortion between certainty and oblivion gave me a kind of vertigo, something of a 'detective' anguish (the theme of *Blow-Up*

was not far off); I went to the photographer's show as to a police investigation, to learn at last what I no longer knew about myself" (85).

2. Robert Bresson, *Notes on Cinematography*, trans. Jonathan Griffin (New York: Urizen Books, 1977), 11.

3. The obturation of the visible was already remarked on in the very syntax of Julio Cortázar's short story "The Devil's Drool" (also known as "Blow-Up," in *Blow-Up and Other Stories*, trans. Paul Blackburn [New York: Collier Books, 1968]), which inspired the film ("inspired by a short story by Julio Cortázar," we read in the credits). Clouds—and pigeons—are the *obturators* of the phrase that narrates (the interruption of) what we see. They are the punctuation of the visible. Thus, "Michel knew that the photographer always worked as a permutation of his personal way of seeing the world as other than the camera insidiously imposed upon it (now a large cloud is going by, almost black), but he lacked no confidence in himself" (103). Or: "I imagined the possible endings (now a small fluffy cloud appears, almost alone in the sky)" (108).

4. On the gaze as the punctuation or phrasing of the image, see my *Of Stigmatology: Punctuation as Experience*, trans. Jan Plug (New York: Fordham University Press, 2017), 5 and 74–81.

5. Roland Barthes, "The Third Meaning: Research Notes on Some Eisenstein Films," in *Image, Music, Text*, trans. Stephen Heath (New York: Harper Collins, 1977), 54, 62. The language is of course that of Bataille's general economy. Bataille is quoted on page 60.

6. The French *obvie*, which has the same Latin origin as the English *obvious*, is a pun on the French title of the volume that contains "The Third Meaning": *L'Obvie et l'obtus.*—Trans.

7. Roland Barthes, "Leaving the Movie Theater," in *The Rustle of Language*, trans. Richard Howard (Berkeley: University of California Press, 1989), 347.

LOCATIONS: 23, RUE BÉNARD, PARIS, 75014

1. I have tried to analyze this possibility, which is linked to a new grid of the visible, in *Kant in the Land of Extraterrestrials: Cosmopolitical Philosofictions*, trans. Will Bishop (New York: Fordham University Press, 2013). It is grounded in a *privatization of vision* (for which Google is one of the principal metonymies); it is the result of taking over, appropriating, the field of perception: what I suggested we call, with and beyond Carl Schmitt, a *nomos of the sensible* (124).

DELETED SCENE: THE FLUCTUATIONS OF THE UNCHAINED CAMERA (L'HERBIER)

1. "They gave me the entire stock exchange for three days," L'Herbier says, "and I used it like a studio": "There were 1,500 extras, about 15 cameramen, scaffolds that went up to the peak of the dome, 40 metres from the

ground . . . and cameras everywhere." See Noël Burch, *Marcel L'Herbier* (Paris: Seghers, 1973), 105.

2. The title of a lecture he gave in 1926, or two years before he began filming *Money*. Deleuze quotes it in the pages from *The Time-Image* I was circling around throughout the first lecture (105). See the passage quoted in Burch, page 98: "The finance I am concerned with, in relation to the Cinematographer, is not an ordinary finance. . . . In essence, it is totally special. Its quoted 'values' are not mining, metallurgy, or transport. They are *more aerial* [my emphasis]. I would even call them metaphysical. To put it plainly, I wanted us to look together at the relationships between cinematography and these two abstract 'values' that dominate all human activity, intellectual and other, from above: 'Time' and 'Space'" (translation modified).

DELETED SCENES: THE GENERAL FETISHISM OF THE MARXES

1. Sigmund Freud, "Fetishism," in *The Standard Edition of the Complete Psychological Works of Sigmund Freud*, vol. 21, trans. James Strachey (London: Hogarth and the Institute of Psychoanalysis, 1971), 147–57.

2. On the history of the word *scotomization* in psychoanalysis from Charcot to Lacan, see Martin Jay, *Downcast Eyes: The Denigration of Vision in Twentieth-Century French Thought* (Berkeley: University of California Press, 1994), 353ff.

3. Paul-Laurent Assoun, *Le Fétichisme* (Paris: Presses Universitaires de France, 1994), 85–86. The idea of a "general fetishism" is already found in Charles de Brosses's *Du Culte des dieux fétiches* (1760; "On the Cult of Fetish Gods," trans. Daniel H. Leonard, in Daniel H. Leonard and Rosalind Morris, *The Returns of Fetishism: Charles de Brosses and the Afterlives of an Idea* [Chicago: University of Chicago Press, 2017]). After discussing the "Yucatan peninsula in America" (56), he declares, "Fetishism is no less widely spread [*général*] in all the regions of America." From the opening pages of his book on (45–46), De Brosses also signals that he is about to generalize from the "the worship . . . of certain terrestrial and material objects called *Fetishes* by the African Negroes, [which] for that reason I will call . . . *Fetishism*":

> I ask that I be permitted to use this expression habitually: though in its proper signification it refers in particular to the beliefs of African Negroes, I signal in advance that I plan to use it equally in speaking of any other nation whatsoever, where the objects of worship are animals, or inanimate beings that are divinized. I will sometimes use it even in talking about certain peoples for whom objects of this sort are not so much Gods, properly speaking, as they are things endowed with a divine virtue: oracles, amulets, and protective talismans. For in general, all these ways of thinking have at bottom the same source, which is merely the appurtenance of a general Religion spread very far over the entire earth, and which must be examined on its own as composing a particular class among the diversity of Pagan Religions.

After De Brosses, we also find the expression *general fetishism* in numerous authors, but always, as in De Brosses himself, to indicate the generalized application of a concept that remains unchanged. Jacques Derrida is the first, to my knowledge, to take this generalization *into* the concept itself, when he writes in *Glas*:

> Despite all the variations to which it can be submitted, the concept fetish includes an invariant predicate: it is a substitute—for the thing itself as center and . . . origin of presence. . . . If what has always been called fetishism, in all the critical discourses, implies the reference to a nonsubstitutive thing, there should be somewhere—and that is the truth of the fetish, the relation of the fetish to truth—a decidable value of the fetish, a decidable opposition of the fetish to the nonfetish. . . . And yet . . . there would be perhaps, particularly in Freud, enough not to make fly into pieces but to reconstruct starting from its generalization a "concept" of fetish that no longer lets itself be contained in . . . the opposition *Ersatz*/non*Ersatz*. (Jacques Derrida, *Glas*, trans. John P. Leavey Jr. and Richard Rand [Lincoln: University of Nebraska Press, 1974], 209)

4. Responding to the opening credits, at the other end of the film, is the phrase *The End*, which is set off from the rapid downward movement in which, one last time, the floors of the department store pass by, this time from top to bottom.

DELETED SCENES: THE AMORTIZATION OF THE GAZE (*KING KONG*)

1. See Theodor W. Adorno, "Mammoth," in *Minima Moralia: Reflections on Damaged Life*, trans. E. F. N. Jephcott (New York: Verso, 1974), 115; and Virginie Despentes, *King Kong Théorie* (Paris: Le Livre de Poche, 2011), 112. In her feminist and postcolonial reading of *King Kong*, E. Ann Kaplan speaks of how "the male gaze and the imperial gaze are linked" (69) and then analyzes this link as a "layering" or "relay" of gazes (71). See Kaplan, *Looking for the Other: Feminism, Film, and the Imperial Gaze* (New York: Routledge, 1997).

2. In her memoirs, Fay Wray says,

> From his vantage point behind the camera, he had perspective and detailed clarity. From my position, all I could see were large blurry shadowy movements on the screen. It was like having the worst seat in the house, too close to define what the shadows were. But I kept moving, kept reacting as though I really could see the fearsome creatures, and would scream when Cooper said, "Scream! Scream for your life, Fay!" (Quoted by Cynthia Erb in *Tracking King Kong: A Hollywood Icon in World Culture* [Detroit: Wayne State University Press, 1998], 39)

3. Jacques Lacan, "Of the Gaze as *Objet petit a*," in *The Four Fundamental Concepts of Psychoanalysis*, ed. Jacques-Alain Miller, trans. Alan Sheridan (New York: Norton, 1978), 82, 109.

FORMATS: SURPLUS DEFINITION (REDACTED)

1. Hito Steyerl, "In Defense of the Poor Image," in *The Wretched of the Screen* (Berlin: Sternberg, 2012), 31–45. The "wretched of the screen" named in the title (playing on the title of Frantz Fanon's famous *The Wretched of the Earth*) are low definition images, what Steyerl calls "poor" images (32):

> The poor image is a copy in motion. Its quality is bad, its resolution substandard. As it accelerates, it deteriorates. . . . Poor images are the contemporary Wretched of the Screen, the debris of audiovisual production, the trash that washes up on the digital economies' shores. They testify to the violent dislocation, transferals, and displacement of images—their acceleration and circulation within the vicious cycles of audiovisual capitalism. (32–33)

When Steyerl then proposes to "redefine the value of the image" (41) according to other criteria, it is nonetheless difficult to see what such a redefinition might consist in. She writes, "Apart from resolution and exchange value, one might imagine another form of value defined by velocity, intensity, and spread. Poor images are poor because they are heavily compressed and travel quickly" (42). But what is this velocity or propagation of an image if not precisely its exchange value? In other words, this "other form of value" Steyerl would like to define is essentially nothing but what Walter Benjamin already called the image's "exhibition value." And Steyerl in fact uses this concept without much rigor when she asserts romantically, "The poor image is . . . a lumpen proletariat in the class society of appearances . . . It transforms quality into accessibility, exhibition value into cult value" (32). The exact opposite would need to be said: In Benjamin's terms, accessibility is exhibition value while quality stems, rather, from the cultic value of an image.

2. Jonathan Sterne, *MP3: The Meaning of a Format* (Durham, N.C.: Duke University Press, 2012), 1–2.

3. If one tries to gather information on the strangely disturbing universe of steganography, one often finds oneself confronted with a frustrating alternative between far-fetched speculations about how "terrorists" supposedly use it and dry technical manuals crammed full of algorithms and tutorials. For example, the following article explaining (in a rather approximate English) how to hide one image inside another one belongs to the second type: Deepesh Rawat and Vijaya Bhandari, "A Steganography Technique for Hiding Image in an Image Using LSB Method for 24 Bit Color Image," *International Journal of Computer Applications* 64, no. 20 (2013): 15–19. In *Steganography in Digital Media: Principles, Algorithms, and Applications* (Cambridge: Cambridge University Press, 2010), Jessica Fridrich traces the first occurrence of the term to Johannes Tirthemius's *Steganographia*, written around 1499 and published much later, in 1606. Musical steganography is a very old process that is already

described by Athanasius Kircher in a chapter of volume 2 of his *Musurgia universalis* (Rome: Ludovico Grignani, 1650), 366ff. There, Kircher mentions different secret musical "alphabets" that associate a given letter with a given note in order to create a "musurgical steganography" (*steganographia musurgica*), that is, literally, a covered over, erased, or crossed out musical writing. In an article that appeared shortly after the attacks of September 11, 2001, the journalist Hervé Morin gave a quick but useful general survey of the history, both ancient and recent, of steganography, even if the information he cites about the messages supposedly sent by Bin Laden would need to be verified:

> What could be more insignificant, on the internet, than a porn site? According to the *USA Today*, Osama Bin Laden might have used certain impious images posted on such sites to transmit his orders in complete secrecy. Quoting unnamed "official sources," the American paper asserted at the beginning of 2001 that the alleged sponsor of several anti-American attacks—among them those of September 11—in the past might also have posted messages on sports forums that were thus transformed into invisible media for plans and information on the targets. This intelligence is considered credible by numerous specialists in digital watermarking. The technique that is said to have been employed, steganography, involves hiding an image in an "innocent" medium. It can, moreover, be combined with cryptography, which hides the meaning of a missive rather than its existence. The result is thus particularly effective. The secret message is first hidden behind its invisibility. If it is discovered, it still has to be decoded, a challenge for the secret services who, in the case of terrorism, have to do both as quickly as possible before the intelligence gathered becomes obsolete. Steganography is in fact as old a practice as spying. Well before invisible ink, Herodotus describes in his *Histories* (V, 35) how a message tattooed on the skull of a slave and then covered over once his hair grows back served as a signal for a revolt against the Persians. . . . The development of computers and the digitization of texts, images, and sounds has refined and automated the use of steganography. Computer language functions through a binary coding made up of 0s and 1s, bits. The mass of numerical information describing an image or sound is such that it easily allows certain of them to be misappropriated without the appearance of the medium being changed perceptibly. (Hervé Morin, "Des messages terroristes peuvent se cacher dans les images de la Toile," *Le Monde*, September 21, 2001)

4. "Brian De Palma on *Redacted*," rottentomatoes.com, November 15, 2007.

5. Emmanuel Burdeau, review of De Palma's film *Redacted*, *Cahiers du cinéma*, 631 (February 2008): 10–11.

6. Ibid.

gaze, the 6, 44, 57–58, 66, 73–74, 93–94, 96, 98, 107, 109–111, 115, 142n44
Godard, Jean-Luc 4, 9–11, 124–25n12, 125n14; *All's Well* 9–10, 125n14; *Passion* 10; *Script for the Film "Passion"* 10–11
Google Maps 100
Gorin, Jean-Pierre 9–10; *All's Well* 9–10

Handlery, Harry 145n61
Hansen, Miriam Bratu 134–35n7
Harvard Project on the City 71, 145n59
Hegel, Georg Wilhelm Friedrich 32–34, 36, 38, 39, 130n3, 132n12; *Phenomenology of Spirit* 32–34, 130n3
Heidegger, Martin 130n1; "European Nihilism" 130n1
Hemmings, David 92
Herlth, Robert 142n41
Herodotus 153n3; *Histories* 153n3
Hitchcock, Alfred 30–32, 40, 66; *Alfred Hitchcock Presents* 30–32; *Rear Window* 66
Hollywood 81–82
Horkheimer, Max 100, 147n65; *Dialectic of Enlightenment* 147n65
host (eucharist) 7–8
Hume, David 123n7
hypermarket 43, 59
Hyppolite, Jean 33, 34, 130n5

icon (*eikōn*) 4, 7
iconoclasts 7–8
iconography 7
iconomy 4, 6–8, 11, 20, 22–23, 24, 25–26, 27, 39–42, 43–44, 57–58, 60, 67, 71, 75, 87, 93, 97–98, 99, 112–14, 123n7, 133n15, 141n35
idea (*eidos*) 128n25
image 4, 7, 22, 39, 40, 53–54, 57–58, 87, 92–98, 99, 123–24n7, 127n20, 139n23, 152n1; flattening of in Bresson 17, 127n20
image-space (*Bildraum*) 51–54, 59–60, 138n21, 138–39n23
incarnation 6–7
inhibition. *See* Freud, Sigmund

innervation 40, 44, 45–51, 73, 75, 100, 133–34n1, 134–35n7, 135–36n9, 136n11, 139–40n26; as electricity 48–50, 137nn14,15, 141n36
inter-images 85

Jackson, Andrew 14
Jackson, Peter 108–11; *King Kong* (2005) 108–11
Jameson, Fredric 70, 144n56
Jay, Martin 150n2
junkspace 73, 146n62
Justinian, Emperor 7

Kaplan, E. Ann 151n1
Kassagi, Henri 16
Kircher, Athanasius 153n3; *Musurgia universalis* 153n3
Klossowski, Pierre 55
Koolhaas, Rem 71, 73, 143n47, 144n51, 145n59, 146n62
Kubrick, Stanley, *Barry Lyndon* 115
Kumler, Aden 124n9

La Bruyère, Jean de 63, 65, 143n46; *Characters* 63
Lacan, Jacques 110, 150n2, 151n3
Lacis, Asja 50
Laërtius, Diogenes 128n25; *Lives and Opinions of Eminent Philosophers* 128n25
Laforgue, René 103
Laplanche, Jean 141n38
Leach, William 144nn51,53
Lefebvre, Jean-Pierre 34, 131n5
Leo III 7
Leonard, Daniel H. 150n3
Leone, Sergio 34–37, 131n8; *My Name is Nobody (Il mio nome è nessuno)* 34–37; "To John Ford" 131n8
Levinson, Barry 81; *What Just Happened?* 81
L'Herbier, Marcel 15, 62, 101–2, 149–50n1; "Le Cinématographe et l'espace" 102; *Money* 101–2, 150n2
listening 3
Losey, Joseph 21

Peter Szendy is David Herlihy Professor of Humanities and Comparative Literature at Brown University. His books include *Of Stigmatology: Punctuation as Experience* and *All Ears: The Aesthetics of Espionage.*

Jan Plug is Professor of English at the University of Western Ontario.

Thinking Out Loud: The Sydney Lectures in Philosophy and Society
Dimitris Vardoulakis, series editor

Stathis Gourgouris, *Lessons in Secular Criticism*
Bonnie Honig, *Public Things: Democracy in Disrepair*
David Wood, *Deep Time, Dark Times: On Being Geologically Human*